IAIN LEVISON put himself through college working as an emergency medical technician. Since then, he has worked as a truck driver, crab fisherman, fish cutter, housepainter, waiter, and bartender. He currently lives in Philadelphia.

ALSO BY IAIN LEVISON

After the Layoffs: A Novel

A
WORKING STIFF'S
MANIFESTO

A
WORKING STIFF'S
MANIFESTO

A MEMOIR OF THIRTY JOBS I QUIT,

NINE THAT FIRED ME,

AND THREE I CAN'T REMEMBER

Iain Levison

RANDOM HOUSE TRADE PAPERBACKS

NEW YORK

Library of Congress Cataloging-in-Publication Data
Levison, Iain.
A working stiff's manifesto: a memoir of thirty jobs I quit, nine that fired me,
and three I can't remember / Iain Levison.
p.   cm.
Originally published: New York: Soho Press, 2002.
ISBN 0-8129-6794-1
1. Levison, Iain.   2. Employees—United States—Biography.   3. Working
class—United States—Biography.   4. Working class—United States—Anecdotes.
5. Working poor—United States—Anecdotes.   6. Displaced workers—United
States—Anecdotes.   7. Career changes—United States—Anecdotes.
8. Occupations—United States—Anecdotes.   9. Unemployed—United States—
Anecdotes.   10. College graduates—Employment—United States—Anecdotes.
11. United States—Economic conditions—1981—2001—Anecdotes.   12. United
States—Social conditions—1980—Anecdotes.   I. Title.
HD8073.L39   A3   2003   305.5'62'092—dc21
[B]   2002036948

For Marion

Acknowledgments

I'd like to thank (in alphabetical order) the following people, who gave me either encouragement or beer money during the writing of this book: Angela Hendrix, Billy Huang, Andrew Langman, Matt Lewis, Faith Manney, Betty Mizgala, Patti Pelrine, Kate Pennell, Larry Platt, Mark Scepansky, Graham Weddington, and, of course, my mother.

A
WORKING STIFF'S
MANIFESTO

BECOMING AN ASSOCIATE

It's Sunday morning and I am scanning the classifieds. There are two types of jobs in here—jobs I'm not qualified
for and jobs I don't want. I'm considering both.

There are pages and pages of the first type—jobs I will never
get. Must know this, must know that. Must be experienced in
this and that, for at least six years, and be fluent in Chinese, and
be able to fly a jet through antiaircraft fire, and have SIX YEARS
experience in open-heart surgery. Starting salary $32,000. Fax
your résumé to Beverly.

Who is Beverly, I wonder, and what does she know that I
don't? She knows she's getting a paycheck, for starters. She can't
do any of the things required for the job, I'm sure, or she would
be doing them, instead of fielding phone calls. If I knew Beverly
on a personal level, could I get a job doing something at her
company? Is that why they don't put Beverly's last name in

there, to discourage would-be stalkers like me from schmooz-
ing up to her in a bar? From finding out details of her personal
life and bumping into her on the subway, after waiting for four
hours, then asking her out for a drink; then, after a night of pas-
sionate sex, offhandedly wonder if they were hiring for anything down at her firm? I continue on down the column,
learning more and more about skills I don't have, about training
I will never get, about jobs needed in fields I never even knew
existed.

Sometimes the Jobs-I-Can't-Do sections contain a hidden
morsel, though. The words "WILL TRAIN" always trigger a
Pavlovian slobbering in any qualified bullshit artist. If they're
going to train you, what difference does it make what you used
to do? "COMPUTER PROGRAMMER, WILL TRAIN." I know
what a computer is. It's one of those TV things with a typewriter
attached by a cord. If they want to train me to program it, fine.
Then I keep reading. This is an ad for a computer school, where
they teach you all about computers for $2,500, then get you a
job data processing, also known as typing, for nine dollars an
hour. I keep looking.

Today, all the WILL TRAINS are for jobs I don't want.
"MOVERS NEEDED, $8/hr. to start. WILL TRAIN. Guaranteed
overtime." This ad is of the second type. Moving furniture isn't
so bad. It's hard work but it has its perks, one of which is you
never need to work out when you're doing it because your muscles are torn to shit at the end of every day. Eight dollars an
hour is low for New York. After taxes that'll leave about six.
Still, I can deal with that. The problem is the guaranteed overtime. They are obviously understaffed and are trying to make it
look like keeping me at work for fourteen hours a day will be
doing me a favor. They'll think because I answered this ad that
I'm going to be enthusiastic about showing up on Sundays and

holidays. "You wanted overtime," they'll crow, "isn't that why you answered the ad?" I move on down the page.

"FISH CUTTERS NEEDED, $12/hr. to start." This is a combination of both types of jobs—a job I don't want and a job I can't do—all wrapped up in one neat little package. I worked for two years as a fish processor in Alaska, so I know a thing or two about fish, but I can't cut them and I don't want to. But I can talk fish with just about anybody. I can bullshit my way through an interview no problem, and by the time they realize I can't cut, I'm already on the payroll. Then they'll either have to teach me or fire me, and firing me will involve admitting a mistake, so teaching me it will be. Twelve dollars an hour. I'm set. Rent will be paid.

There's a definite trick to applying for jobs for which you are not qualified. Knowing something is key, even if it is just one little fact that you can throw out. You can usually get these facts by listening to boring people. I once spent five hours on a train down to Florida listening to the guy in the next seat ramble on about the woes of house painting, and two days later I was painting houses in Miami after wowing the interviewer with a verbatim rendition of the speech I had just heard. So, with fish I'm set. Just a few mentions of salmon fishing in Alaska, and I'm in.

Another fact about interviewers is that most interviewers just want to hear themselves talk. In the average job interview, I'm usually lucky if I can get a word in edgewise. Interviewers have a captive audience who want something from them, so they can babble away uninterrupted about their restaurant, their business, their life, their opinion of the president, or any subject on their mind. Who's going to disagree with them? It's the perfect dictator's forum. "No, sir, actually I think the President's doing a fine job," and my application is ripped to shreds the minute

I'm gone. I've sat quietly while interviewers tell me facts about their wives, their careers, their golf handicaps, even their first sexual experiences. And they rarely ask anything about me.

I go down to the fish store and we talk fish. This is a high-end fish store, catering to the eclectic needs of housewives from the best areas of New York, I am told. The manager, John, needs someone with a "good attitude," who is "presentable." An ass-kisser with a good haircut. It's the same thing everyone wants, every business from IBM to the local transmission shop. I happen to have a good haircut, and I am relentlessly polite, at least for the first five minutes I meet someone. He tells me to come back tomorrow for orientation, wearing khaki pants and a blue shirt. No questions about fish cutting ability are ever asked.

I have a job. Here we go again.

In the last ten years, I've had forty-two jobs in six states. I've quit thirty of them, been fired from nine, and as for the other three, the line was a little blurry. Sometimes it's hard to tell exactly what happened, you just know it wouldn't be right for you to show up anymore.

I have become, without realizing it, an itinerant worker, a modern-day Tom Joad. There are differences, though. If you asked Tom Joad what he did for a living, he would say, "I'm a farmworker." Me, I have no idea. The other difference is that Tom Joad didn't blow $40,000 getting an English degree.

And the more I travel and look around for work, the more I realize that I am not alone. There are thousands of itinerant workers out there, many of them wearing business suits, many doing construction, many waiting tables or cooking in your favorite restaurants. They are the people who were laid off from companies that promised them a lifetime of security and then changed their minds, the people who walked out of commencement with a $40,000 fly swatter in their hands and got rejected from twenty interviews in a row, then gave up. They're the people who thought, *I'll just take this temporary assignment/bartending job/parking lot attendant position/pizza delivery boy job until something better comes up,* but something better never does, and life becomes a daily chore of dragging yourself into work and waiting for a paycheck, which you can barely use to survive. Then you listen in fear for the sound of a cracking in your knee, which means a $5,000 medical bill, or a grinding in your car's engine, which means a $2,000 mechanic's bill, and you know then that it's all over, you lose. New car loans, health insurance, and mortgages are out of the question. Wives and children are unimaginable. It's surviving, but surviving sounds dramatic, and this life lacks drama. It's scraping by.

It wasn't supposed to be like this. There was a plan once, but over the years I've forgotten what it was. It involved a house and a beautiful wife and a serviceable car and a fenced-in yard, and later a kid or two. Then I'd sit back and write the Great American Novel. There was an unspoken agreement between me and the Fates that, as I lived in the richest country in the history of the world, and was a fairly hard worker, all these things would just come together eventually. The first dose of reality was the military. I remember a recruiter coming to my house, promising to train me in the marketable skill of my choice, which back then was electronics. I remember the recruiter nodding vigorously and describing all the electronics that the army was currently using. They would train me and train me, he said.

This was my first hands-on experience with an experienced corporate bullshit artist. They trained me and trained me all right. Mostly, they trained me to use a rifle and to interrogate Russian and East German prisoners. These are skills that very few electronics firms are in need of. But surely, speaking Russian and German comes in handy, no? No, actually. Not if your main strengths in the language concern tanks and troop movements. Once we get past "Where is your artillery?", a phrase that doesn't come up much in everyday conversation, I'm pretty much lost in either language.

Then there was college. The conventional wisdom is that you are unemployable without a college degree. That you are often unemployable with one is something a lot of people spend a lot of money to discover. An English degree qualifies you for either secretarial work (typing those papers gets your fingers plenty of practice) or teaching English, an irony that seems lost on most English professors I talk to. This is a field that exists to duplicate itself, and, of course, to provide star athletes with legitimate courses they can take on their way to NBA and NFL careers so that they can "attend" college and earn passing grades.

So that's how I wind up here. No wife, no serviceable car, no fenced-in yard. I've obeyed the rules, done my time, and I'm right back where I started—an inch above the poverty line with no hope in sight. Instead of my house and beautiful wife, I've got a tiny one-bedroom New York City apartment, which, for financial reasons, I have to share with a roommate who makes a first-year frat boy look like Martha Stewart.

But before I start my new job, I have promised a day's labor to Corey, my roommate. Corey is in much the same boat as I am, only he had the good sense to drop out of college the minute he became disgusted with it, which was after six weeks. So when the Student Loan people call, it's usually for me.

After his brief college experience, Corey came to New York to work in the film industry, imagining himself shooting up the glamorous ladder of success to become a director. He did direct a small film, an independent production, and the experience left him so drained that now he barely has the energy or enthusiasm to do carpentry work on other directors' movie sets. "You wouldn't believe the bullshit," he tells me. I'm sure I'd believe every word of it. Most of his time and energy was taken up not with camera angles and script supervision, but with trying to get cops not to tow his car every time he set up on a street corner to shoot a scene. Waiting in line to obtain permits, paying parking tickets, and giving money to homeless people to keep other homeless people from jumping in front of the camera is what filmmaking is really about, he explains.

He has recovered somewhat from that experience and is assistant-directing another small film being shot down in Tribeca, and he needs warm bodies to use as gophers. For a chance to see a real movie being shot, I offer my services.

He has gone down to the shoot at four in the morning, and I take the subway down there at about nine. On the way, I make a mistake and read the script I have been asked to bring, which Corey forgot in his early rush. It is awful. Not just run of the mill awful, but not *Plan Nine From Outer Space* awful either, which would have at least made it interesting. This script just sucks. It seems to have been written by someone who watched a lot of television growing up, and instead of incorporating reality into their adult imagination, this writer just incorporated the clichéd images of 1970s television. The drama scenes are from *Mannix* and the love scenes from *The Love Boat*. I can't imagine how this wretched crap made it to the filming stage.

I get to the shoot and realize that nobody wants to hear my opinion of the script because it's already past nine o'clock and they have to finish shooting by nightfall. Corey has only been able to close off the street for one day, and nothing is being done because the sound man is having all kinds of technical glitches.

Corey, who is usually soft-spoken and calm, is buzzing around and screaming at people. I've never seen him like this before. He comes over to me. "Carry these things upstairs," he tells me. He points at a pile of heavy objects that look complex and electronic.

I start to pick one up and the sound man screams, "WHAT THE HELL ARE YOU DOING?"

"He told me to . . ."

"LEAVE MY SHIT ALONE!"

Whoa, Buddy. "Okay," I say softly. I put the expensive thing down gently and stand there. The sound man turns back to what he was doing, and Corey, who created the whole scene, is off to "organize" something else.

These people like to shriek at each other. Scenes like this are a constant of the film trade, I soon learn. In the next few minutes, I see a different sound man shrieking at his assistant, a stuntman nearly attack two passers-by, and the director make loud, snide remarks to a pretty girl who is holding a clipboard. No one here has any social grace or sense of courtesy. They are artistes. They have no responsibilities to the outside world because it is their job to critique it. How could they perform their invaluable task of providing commentary on society if they burden themselves with its restrictive rules?

The sound man comes over to me and hands me a pole. "Take this upstairs," he says without looking at me.

Normally I'd have punched this guy by now, but I'm supposed to be helping Corey, and I don't want to create yet another time delay on his set by injuring someone who knows what's going on. I take it upstairs. There the two "stars," one of whom I actually recognize from a mid 80s sitcom, are going over their dialogue. They look annoyed at my intrusion but don't say anything. I put the pole down and start to leave.

"Hey, bring me up some coffee," the sitcom guy says.

"Me too," says the girl.

"Sure thing," I say. I have no intention of bringing either of them anything because they didn't say "please," but I'm cleared of responsibility when I get downstairs because the lighting guy gives me a mile of wire to untangle. I sit and untangle wire for a bit, then everybody starts getting wildly excited and screaming, "Quiet, quiet!" We're actually going to start filming now. Everybody is still. Then the actress opens the door and comes outside and closes the door.

"Cut!" screams the director.

That was it. That was the result of four hours of preparation, watching this girl open and close a door. Then she does it six more times to get the shot right. Apparently there's a right and wrong way to open and close a door in Hollywood. This must be what you learn in acting school.

"Hey, you, come here," says the sound guy when the excitement is over. I just stare at him. I've read the script, these people are wasting their time. This is a shit movie that would be lucky to wind up in the discount bin of a video store in the Philippines. Maybe if we were filming some masterpiece that was going to change the whole world of film, I'd come running, but my commitment to this project is straining. I know the sound guy probably came here a few years ago, dreaming of working on such a film, and this is his dose of reality. He's just happy to be working, playing with his microphones and miles of wire and getting paid for it. This is his Great Compromise. I've made my own, and it doesn't include being spoken to like that.

Corey, the lighting guy, the actors, they've all given up. This crap film is to them what applying for a job at a fish counter is to me. But here, there is some unwritten rule that you can't admit that you've given up. A very strict rule. Rule One: Whatever you do, never stop bullshitting yourself that you're important. Rule One keeps a lot of people sane.

I've had enough of this. I walk past the soundman, down to the coffee shop at the end of the street, buy myself a cup, and only myself, and sit with the crowd, watching the production from the steps.

On my way home, I call my ex-girlfriend to tell her not to bother coming to visit the glamorous world of film. I'd invited her down to the shoot, hoping that she might find a glimpse of filmmaking fascinating enough to reconsider her recent decision to seek a boyfriend elsewhere. My inability to hold a shitty job while working on the Great American Novel was causing strain on our relationship. I'd come home from jobs waiting tables or moving furniture and be too tired to write, and my lack of literary output had her convinced that my writing dream was just a line that I'd used to pick her up in the first place.

"Van Gogh painted when he was broke," she told me once. "People can do things when they're broke."

Van Gogh ruined it for the rest of us. Sane people who want a career in the arts want a halfway decent life while they examine the deeper issues. There's no image there, though. It's all about image. Most people who can't name two of Van Gogh's paintings know that he was a starving nutcase. He sat in a corner and poured out art while his food supply ran out and people came to evict him. Now that was an artist. Cut off his ear and mailed it to a woman. Now that's passion. Actually, it's schizophrenia. I'd hoped not to model myself on a schizophrenic self-mutilator who died in obscurity, but any argument of mine was just a rationale for lack of commitment to my trade.

It turns out she wasn't coming anyway. She'd gone to lunch with some guy from the office.

The Market, where I am now employed as a fish cutter, is a grocery store that tries to combine rustic charm with nonrustic prices. It sports a bakery, a kitchen, an espresso stand, even a flower shop. You can buy anything you'll ever need here, providing all you'll ever need is overpriced haute cuisine, espresso, and flowers.

There is a trend afoot among businesses these days to complicate things, then give the product of all their complications a simple name. The Market conjures up images of farmers hawking their produce in a warehouse, with chickens squawking in the background and cornhusks and other vegetable debris littered around a sawdust floor. Nothing could be further from the truth. The Market where I am employed has been meticulously pieced together, every detail the result of careful market research. The bathroom is placed behind the meat counter to discourage users (who wants to see animal guts?) and the quick items, the milk, and the bread, which people might want to just grab and dash out with are conveniently placed all the way at the back of the store. This way, the shopper will have to walk past every item while inhaling the aromas of freshly baked bread and cinnamon-laced cappuccino, increasing the willingness to spend.

As I suspected from the job interview, appearances are key. The general manager, Zoe, comes down to say hello to me as I sift through the introductory paperwork in the break room on my first day. She gives me a quick professional smile and shakes my hand as she nods approvingly at my khaki pants. "Very nice," she murmurs. Then she looks with consternation at my blue shirt.

"Is that an oxford?"

"What's an oxford?"

"The shirt. Is it an oxford shirt?"

"I don't know. Is it?"

"You need an oxford."

"Okay."

She nods approvingly at my pants again. "Very nice," she says. "But you have to have an oxford."

I give her the thumbs-up on the oxford issue and a big smile, and she walks off, confident that the next time she sees me I will be wearing an oxford shirt. This is one of her duties, to make sure everyone wears an oxford. Over the years, I've noticed that employers who are sensible in almost every respect often have no flexibility or sense of humor when it comes to uniforms. It could be something they are taught in business courses in college, that the uniform represents the company, that it has to be worn with pride, that a soiled or poor-appearing employee is the first unraveling of a tightly wound organization. I'm not so sure, though. I think that abusing people about their appearance is an easy and convenient way for managers to show off their power.

Think about it. In what other possible situation can one person reasonably say to another that ultimate power comment, "You look like shit." In the army, I once saw a man forced to do pushups because he had missed a tiny patch of skin when he was shaving, and we understood this was part of the abuse of training. We were expecting abuse and we got it. The working world is no different, except that the comments are phrased slightly differently, and are accompanied by a distant power-smile and a handshake. Of course sometimes, though rarely, uniform comments are necessary. I was an EMT in Philadelphia and I worked with a guy who looked like he slept in his car every night, and he smelled like it too.

But today my blue button-down nonoxford shirt was ironed to perfection and I smelled sweet as summer rain. What Zoe doesn't realize is that the next time she sees me, I'll be wearing this shirt, and the time after that too. Nothing personal, it's just that I can't afford a new shirt until I get paid, and I'm not getting a paycheck for at least a week, perhaps two, and this is the only blue shirt I have. I doubt I'll get fired over it, though it's more likely that I'll get fired for that than for the fact that I'm completely incapable of performing the job I was hired to do.

I got lucky on the khaki pants. I actually owned a pair of nice ones, worth about fifty dollars, and now they're about to get splattered with fish guts.

Zoe is gone. I sit in the employee break room and read propaganda about the company I have just joined. The Market, I learn, has branches wherever there are people with money to burn. Wherever there are people driving up half-mile driveways in sport-utility vehicles, we are there. There are branches in Beverly Hills, Long Island (about five different stores), Grosse Point, the Main Line, and so on. The company headquarters is in Maryland. All sexual harassment complaints and personal disputes must be filed with the Maryland office, and a list of phone numbers for that purpose is provided. It is tossed in the trash. Whatever else they can say about me, I'm not a squealer. Besides, I've only ever known two people to call an 800 number to complain about sexual harassment, and both were fired as troublemakers.

Then I flip through a sixteen-page document entitled "Becoming an Associate," and am on page three before I realize that associate means employee. The mangling of the English language has become commonplace in the corporate world, and people who work at the Market's lowest-level jobs are all given titles. Thus, I am encouraged to tell my friends about exciting career openings as a chef's assistant (vegetable chopper or dishwasher, depending on the chef's needs at the time), sales records associate (checkout girl), or sanitation maintenance associate (janitor). An enclosed flyer tells me that I will be awarded fifty dollars for each person I can bring to the company. Small print, about a page of it, describes the conditions that have to be met before the check is handed over. The employee must stay ninety days, I must still be employed by the company after the employee's ninety days, the employee must be highly rated, a request for the check must go through headquarters in Maryland, and on and on. Lawyers know that most people would rather sign their rights away than read page after page of small print, and the people who devised this bounty system, as it is called, probably did so with the same mentality. Most of us would rather kiss fifty dollars good-bye than bother with any more legalese. I flip the page and read on.

After ninety days, I am eligible for insurance. That's always a nice one. That the insurance costs twenty-five dollars a week and doesn't really cover anything except lightning bolt strikes is something that only people with the patience to read the aforementioned legalese will ever find out. There is also a profit-sharing program, in which associates get a Christmas bonus of stock in their name every year, provided they have been there one year or longer. The amount of stock increases every year that the associate is with the company. Promises of great wealth for long-term employees are not unusual at businesses with high turnover, where the management knows that little, if any, of the promised wealth will ever have to be distributed. Benefits for short-term employees, things I could actually use now, such as free meals and paid breaks, are never to be found.

John, the fish counter manager, comes into the break room to see how I am doing with the paperwork. "All done?"

I have barely started. There are almost fifty pages of small print to go in the introduction manual alone. I have just started on the chapter about how it can all end, called "Associate Abuses and Termination." Here I am told that bringing a gun or drugs to work will get me fired, as will stealing, or "any other felony." Lying is also mentioned as a grounds for dismissal. Apparently, I am not allowed to lie to other associates, which negates one of my hobbies. There are just enough broad-ended generalities in there to indicate that they can fire me if they don't like me. Of course, there's an 800 number to call if I feel that has happened, but I imagine if I do that, I get caught up in a paperwork conspiracy so endless that it would be better to just get another job.

"There's a lot of paperwork here," I tell him. "Might be a while."

"Just fill out the tax stuff and throw the rest away," he says, then quickly corrects himself. "Or take it home." He looks at his watch. "We need to get going. We have to unload the truck."

Unload the truck. Now I see why I got through the interview so easily. I'm over six feet tall and appear to have considerable lifting power.

I pull seventy-pound boxes off the refrigerated delivery truck and realize that it might not have been my fine haircut or charm that got me the job. John was sizing me up like a medieval lord looking at a prospective new serf, checking me for labor potential. As I unload the truck, John tells me stories about how hard he has worked, ever since he was a teenager, in the meat and fish industry. He is a few years older than me. When he was twenty-one, he bought the meat and fish store from the man who taught him the business, and ran it up until a year ago, when he came to work for the Market. He is unclear about what happened to his store, or why he found working here preferable. He mentions that he is a type-A personality, a workaholic who just can't stop himself. He tells me this as he watches me, hands in his pockets, barely looking at the ice-filled Styrofoam boxes of fish he is supposed to be checking for quality. He is more interested in the weather, reminiscing, and the tightly-clad women we can see going into the store's front entrance. It's only my first day with him, but he appears to have come to terms with his workaholism.

We go back inside, and I am introduced to the junior manager, an Italian fellow named Ippolito. Ippolito is making the schedule for the fish department. It turns out there are only three people who work the fish counter, and I am the third, which explains my rapid and untested hiring. I thought they were looking for an ass-kisser with a good haircut, and it turns out they wanted someone, anyone. These two chiefs were obviously desperate for an Indian. I become more confident of my status.

As I am putting the crates away in the freezer, I hear pieces of a conversation between Ippolito and John. Ippolito is asking for a raise, I gather, and John is hemming and hawing. I shut the freezer door so they won't think I'm eavesdropping. I've seen this scene before, and I already know how this is going to turn out.

When the fish has been neatly stacked in the freezer, I come outside, and Ippolito is alone, filleting flounder. I watch his hands, trying to pick up silent pointers on fish cutting. No doubt he has done this before. His nimble hands remove the meat from the bones of each fish with a few deft strokes. When I look up, I realize his cheeks are flushed with rage.

"How much you make?" he asks me, still cutting the fish. He has a thick Italian accent but his English is good. "How much they pay you?"

There's no way around it. It's a direct question, and I figure he's a manager, he's entitled to the information. "Twelve dollars an hour."

"Motherfucker," he says. "That motherfucker."

I nod sympathetically.

"You cut fish good? You better than me?"

"Uh, no."

"But you cut fish before, right?"

"Sure." Worst comes to worst, I can always claim a blow to the head or carpal tunnel syndrome to explain my suddenly lost abilities.

"You cut flounder good?"

"Flounder . . . that's always been a problem for me."

"Because they are flat, right? Flat fish are hard." Ippolito is smiling now, enjoying the brotherhood of us fishcutters, those who know that flat fish are hard. He hands me the knife. "Cut me a flounder."

It's go time. I've seen him do at least ten of them, and I have a built in excuse—flat fish are hard—so I dive right in. I pull a flounder out of the box, insert the knife under the skin the same way I have seen him do it ten times, and the knife strikes a bone right away. I wriggle it around, but I can't get the knife away from the bone.

"Here, let me show you." My secret is out, and Ippolito seems to have expected it. He slowly inserts the knife, makes a few deft movements, and lifts the meat from the bones. Like magic. He hands me another flounder, and again I strike bone.

"You cut fish before?" he asks again.

"Sure. In Alaska. Long time ago."

"Alaska fish, maybe they are different," he says, his voice fatherly and kind. A light goes on as I suddenly realize the situation. Ippolito knows damned well Alaskan fish and Atlantic fish are pretty much the same. He's not a bad guy, I figure. He knows I can't do the job, but I imagine they've been working him to death the last few weeks, especially if he was teamed with Workaholic John, and he just wants some time off. He's willing to work with me just to keep me here. After all, I'm polite and I have a good haircut. And if I turn out to be a complete fuck-up, hell, he didn't hire me, John did.

And so I'm in.

Ippolito spends several hours showing me how to cut fish, and he tells me his life story. He's been cutting fish since he was a kid, growing up in a small fishing village in Italy. He came to America three years ago, married an American girl, and got a job cutting fish here in Scarsdale, New York.

They hired Ippolito at eight dollars an hour, probably because he couldn't speak English very well back then. Despite the fact that he is now almost fluent, his wages haven't gone up that much. Two years later, he now makes eleven. Then they hired me for twelve.

Instead of giving him a raise, John then decided to give Ippolito a title, junior manager. The responsibilities consist of making the schedule for one person, me. Basically, his managerial perk is to schedule me whenever he doesn't want to work, but he is limited because he is still getting an hourly wage. He needs to give himself a decent living, and he can't give me overtime. The Market is not going to give me eighteen dollars an hour to mangle fish. In fact, they're not going to give me eighteen dollars an hour for anything, ever. They have some kind of computer system, I am told, where lights and buzzers go off in the payroll office the minute anyone receives overtime, and regional managers and district managers and various other executives fly in from the golf course and start screaming. So Ippolito's big perk is to schedule me Sunday mornings, which he has been working for the last two years, and now he can finally go to church with his wife.

Ippolito is a loyal, competent, hardworking man and I am an incompetent drifter making more money than he is. The

Market will eagerly pay security guards to watch monitors on six-figure security systems to make sure that we don't steal three-dollar bottles of salad dressing, but they won't give this man the money he deserves, even when he politely asks for it. To them it is a game. How little can we get him to work for? Poor wop, barely speaks English, let's crap on his head from a great height. Ah, look, our best employee makes less than that haircut we just hired, let's make him a manager. And everything is all right. Ippolito's wife is pregnant; he's not going anywhere. I don't have a wife, and no one else wants my job, so I get anything I want.

I respect Ippolito for knowing he is getting screwed, and I respect him more for mentioning it to me. A lot of people in his situation would abuse me because I got lucky. He could spend all day complaining to John about how incompetent I am, trying to get me fired, but where would that leave him? Working Sunday mornings again. Then the Market would eventually hire someone else, maybe someone who cuts fish as well as he does, and then he'd have to feel threatened about losing his manager position. Me, I'm a nice, easy-going guy, I do what I'm told, I work Sunday mornings, and best of all, I'm incompetent. I'm no threat to anyone. I'm fitting in nicely.

The next few days go by peacefully. By my second day, I am trusted to run the entire fish counter by myself. Ippolito comes in at seven, cuts most of the fish, and leaves at three o'clock. The Market closes at seven, and there is an hour of closing duty, so both of us manage an eight-hour shift. Best of all, I only have to spend the first three hours of my shift with a supervisor. After that, I am on my own.

Like most modern itinerant workers, I've waited tables for long enough to be proficient at customer service, and am soon on the fast track to success at the Market. Zoe comes by and notices me chatting amiably with some regulars, who make a point of telling her what a splendid individual I am. She doesn't even mention that I am still wearing the same shirt she told me to exchange during our first meeting. After nine days, I get my first paycheck, over $400 for a forty-hour week, and rush out and buy an oxford. I'm one of the team.

My regular customers take to me. One of them brings me a pen, an expensive ink pen with elegant designs on it. He owns a company that makes them, he tells me. Later in the day, I am over at the coffee stand and notice that the Market sells those pens. Maybe his company sells them to the Market, or maybe the guy's just bringing me some of the Market's stock as a gift. I don't know. At any rate, it's the thought that counts.

A few evenings later, I'm minding my own business behind the fish stand. It has been a slow day, a clock-watching day, and I am eating a chocolate bar while doing inventory. Zoe comes back behind the stand.

"Hi," she says brusquely. "Where'd you get that chocolate bar?"

"I bought it," I say. I have carefully read the Market policy on eating lunch and taking breaks and cigarette smoking, all of which they'd prefer you didn't do, but if you must, there are ten pages of guidelines on exactly how. I know them all by heart. I'm a lunch-eating, break-taking, cigarette-smoking machine, seeing as I'm stuck back here in a very unbusy store by myself for eight hours at a time. I know that all items bought from the store by employees during their shift have to be accompanied by a receipt. "I have my receipt right here."

She nods without looking at it. "Where did you get this pen?"

"A customer gave it to me."

"He gave it to you?" Her eyes narrow with suspicion.

"He said he owns the factory where they're made."

"This is one of our pens."

"He gave it to me."

"Do you have a receipt?"

"He didn't give me one."

She looks at me as if I am the worst-lying pen-stealer she has ever encountered, and shrugs and walks off.

After that, things go downhill quickly. The next day, we get a rare rush, seven or eight people at the stand at a time. I have everything organized, waiting on people as quickly as I can. They have formed a line, and I get them one at a time. Zoe comes up to the stand.

"Wait on that lady," she tells me, pointing at an ill-tempered older woman, as I am wrapping an order for the lady in front of her. I assume Zoe will finish wrapping the order, so I put it down and approach the next lady.

"Can I help you?" I ask the ill-tempered one.

"Yes, I'd like two pounds of salmon steak."

"Hey!" yells the one I was just waiting on. I look around and realize that Zoe has wandered away, but is still watching me. The lady's unwrapped order is sitting where I left it. I go over and start wrapping again.

"Why did you ask me if you could help me before you were finished with her?" howls the ill-tempered one.

"All I want is my order," the one waiting for the wrapped package cries out with exaggerated patience. Other ladies at the back of the line start rolling their eyes and wandering off.

After it is quiet again, Zoe comes up to me. "I don't think you should be alone back here," she tells me. "You can't handle it by yourself. I'll tell Ippolito." She looks at me a moment. "Is that an oxford?"

I'm not sure exactly what I've done to draw her attention, but she's got her teeth in and she won't let go. She starts with me on a daily basis.

"You'd better get back there," she tells me one day when I'm going out to smoke. "We've got customers coming in."

I've been back there for five hours and sold one piece of fish. I have already asked one of the butchers to watch my stand for a few minutes. We take turns. When I come back, he goes.

"Rocker's back there," I say.

"I'd feel more comfortable if you were back there too."

I go back. Smokers are always fair game. Rocker smokes his cigarette in the freezer with all the meat. I still care, just enough, to decide this is unsanitary. It's also freezing.

Rocker the butcher has been putting up with Zoe for over a year, and he doesn't care about anything anymore. He is a lifetime butcher who recently lost his own business to bankruptcy, and Zoe has been trying to get him fired since John hired him. He doesn't say "Have a nice day" enough and never wears an oxford.

That night, Rocker and I start closing the displays down at ten to eight. Zoe comes over and screams, "Eight o'clock! That's when we close! Eight o'clock! Refill the ice tubs!"

I have already emptied two ten-gallon ice tubs, and she wants me to refill them for the final ten minutes of the shift. This involves going downstairs to the ice machine, a process that takes ten minutes. By the time I'm done, it will be eight o'clock.

I shrug and go downstairs and refill the ice tubs and throw the ice away as soon as I have returned to the fish stand.

"Good," she says.

"It's just going to get worse," Rocker says, while he takes a wrapped pork loin, slides it down his pants, and winks at me.

And so I learn to steal stuff.

I've been there long enough to know where the cameras are, and I devise a system. One of my jobs is to use leftover fish to make free samples of various dishes, which I leave out for the customers to give them ideas on how the fish can be prepared. This job requires that I wander around the store and take items off the shelves, sauces and marinades, and take them back behind the counter, away from the cameras, to use in the preparation of the dish.

I wander around the store and grab anything I can get my hands on. I grab soy sauce, bags of coffee beans, yogurt, chocolate bars, more pens, and stockpile them in the back at the end of each shift. I grab tape, staples, even fish knives.

Most of all, I grab fish. I wrap one-pound chunks of Chilean sea bass up in three layers of plastic and stuff it down my pants every night on my way out the door. Rule one is nothing ever goes in my duffel bag. Management reserves the right to search the duffel bag at any time. Everything goes down the pants.

Before long, Corey and I are eating sixteen-dollar-a-pound sea bass and salmon like it's a bag of Doritos. We have langostinos in cream sauce, lobster tails on a bed of saffron rice, Pacific red salmon and Alaskan king crab legs mixed with jumbo Maryland scallops, a gigantic seafood extravaganza served on a nightly basis. Soon my roommate is begging for burgers. So I talk to Rocker and arrange a trade-off at the butcher stand. We go to two-inch-tall cuts of New York strip steak, filet mignon, big wads of hamburger meat, dry-aged rib eye, even a rare cut of Kobe beer-fed beef. Every time Zoe makes a comment to me that I deem to be less than positive, more things go down the pants.

I start noticing how many other Market employees feel the same way. While waiting for the train, I listen to them bitch about their jobs. They've all been made to read one directive too many, about oxfords and hair length and "Have a nice day." They are all getting paid a different wage for the same job, and there's no reasoning behind it. People are promoted based on nothing. A sweet nineteen-year-old girl is promoted to head cashier after two weeks, leaving the others seething. I wonder if they all have pants stuffed with stolen groceries.

Ippolito, I notice, starts giving me the cold shoulder. Obviously, Zoe is riding him about me, and he takes to snapping at me. A customer calls and orders poached salmon, and I get the water boiling, and Ippolito comes in and starts screaming.

"I cook the salmon," he tells me. "I cook all special orders."

"Knock yourself out."

"From now on, I cook all the orders."

"Fine."

Later that day, just before Ippolito leaves, I start getting scrap fish together for a soy and sesame display I have planned. Cooking fish is one of the things I'm good at. Most of the customers like my samples.

"I'll do it," he says. He takes the scraps without looking at me. "From now on, I do the cooking."

"Do it up." He stays around an extra half hour, waiting for his samples to come out of the oven. Even then he doesn't leave. Zoe apparently has instructed him to keep an eye on me. I am getting twelve dollars an hour to stare into space.

After he has left, I am sitting at the desk behind the fish counter, and I open a drawer looking for tape to date the scallops. I see the next schedule. I am not on it. A guy named Roberto is.

The next day is the last day of the scheduled week. Usually, they have posted the schedule by now. I spend most of my shift wandering around the store, looking for expensive stuff. I find a thirteen-dollar can opener, the cutting edge of can openers, with round black rubber grips. I take two of them, pop them down my pants, and go out to smoke a cigarette. I throw them into a bush.

I grab more can openers, smoke again. I grab chocolate bars, expensive German chocolate, duck back behind the fish counter and load my socks with it, then go and smoke. Into the bush. I double wrap about four pounds of sockeye salmon and smoke again. When I come back inside, John is waiting for me.

"Can I talk to you for a second?"

"Sure."

"I hired a guy yesterday. Eight dollars an hour. He can cut fish. I don't think we're going to have room for you here anymore."

"Sure."

"It's nothing personal."

"It's fine."

"Come with me." He escorts me to my locker, which I clean out while he watches. Once you've been dismissed, there is a Market policy that a manager has to be with you all the time, to prevent theft or unsightly displays of emotion. He escorts me outside.

"I'm going to have to look in your bag," he says. He takes it from me. I have a book and a t-shirt inside. He hands it back. "You were always an honest guy," he says. "It's just a policy."

"No problem."

"So long."

I shake his hand, circle the block, and load up on can openers, fish, and chocolate. The irony is that after three months at the Market, I have become a half-decent fish cutter.

My insurance would have kicked in after ninety days. I have worked there eighty-nine.

"What're these?" I am emptying my bag onto the kitchen counter, looking at my legacy from the Market. Corey is examining the contents, disappointed. He'd been expecting sea bass.

"Can openers."

"Where'd you get 'em?"

"A friend gave 'em to me."

"Why'd he give you nine can openers?"

"Do you want 'em or not?"

"Not really."

Maybe I'll sell them. Maybe not. I don't have a gift for sales. Back to the classifieds.

Corey has to leave town that night on a shoot, and just minutes after he walks out he gets a phone call from a woman in Scarsdale, which I am lucky enough to intercept.

"I'm desperate," she tells me. "I need you."

I'm wondering what she looks like when I remember that, for the last several weeks, Corey has had an ad in the paper for a private bartending service to make extra money. Some months back, he answered an ad for a bartender, which turned out to be a cleverly worded ad for a bartending *school*, and, too embarrassed to admit his mistake, he'd shelled out $1,000 to learn how to make Golden Cadillacs and Harvey Wallbangers. By the time he'd realized that most of the people who drink these drinks are dead, the check had been cashed. Now he felt obligated to try to get himself some bartending work to recoup the cash.

Her name is Patrice and she is throwing a party at her Scarsdale mansion for a hundred or so of her influential friends, and she has had a last minute falling-out with her caterer. I feel her pain. I hate when that happens. Anyway, Patrice needs a bartender for tomorrow evening, someone to stand around and pour bottles of Chateau Whatever for her apéritif-sipping friends. I get the feeling there will be little skill and plenty of subservience required. I can do subservience for an evening, especially considering my current employment status.

"Do you have a cummerbund?" she asks. This apparently is a key requirement.

"Of course," I say. What unemployed guy doesn't have a cummerbund?

"And a bow tie?"

"Sure."

She gives me the address and some directions, and we agree on four o'clock the next day.

I go rummaging through Corey's stuff, figuring that anyone who places a bartending ad is going to have a cummerbund and bow tie handy. If he does, he's got them well hidden. So I have to go downtown and buy these two things at the only place I can find them, which is a high-end men's clothing store. The cheapest possible alternatives cost me thirty-six dollars so I figure that I'll just wear them for that night and then take them back the next day.

"Make sure you've got the right ones," the sales girl tells me. "Absolutely no returns."

"Sure. No problem." Fuck. Maybe I can sell them to Corey.

The next day, I take the train out to Scarsdale (three dollars each way) and the cab to her house from the station (eight dollars each way), and I realize as I'm walking up her driveway that I've already laid out fifty-eight dollars on this affair. I'm getting fifteen-dollars an hour and am expected to work four hours, so I'm now looking at a two-dollar profit margin for the entire evening. Fuck it. It'll be easy work, and I'm jobless, so I have nothing else to do. And who knows, maybe I'll meet a guy who owns a publishing firm or a nymphomaniac heiress whose husband is out of town.

The first person I meet is Patrice. She's probably okay under normal circumstances, but arranging this party has stressed the normalcy right out of her. She's running around in circles talking to herself, stopping every now and then to scream at a teenage boy, who, it turns out, is her neighbor's son. He's setting up a table to shuck steamed oysters on. She comes over to me.

"You must be Corey," she says. Corey's ad had his name in it, and before I can correct her, she starts off with a barrage of instructions. I'm to set up a long card table on the patio, cover it with a table cloth, then arrange dozens of bottles of liquor, wine, and mixers as attractively as possible. Easy enough. While I'm doing this, she comes by every few minutes to micro-manage, move a few bottles around, adjust the tablecloth length, but other than that she leaves me alone. I get finished early and help the kid set up the oyster table. He is going to be shucking oysters while I pour wine.

"Getting cold out," he observes.

I've started to notice that myself. Since I left Manhattan, the temperature has dropped about thirty degrees. I get my coat out of my bag and bundle up, thanking God that I brought my coat, which I did only as an afterthought as I was walking out the door, just in case the night turned chilly.

Guests begin to arrive as a light dusting of snow starts to fall, mixing intermittently with freezing rain, which makes the smooth-stoned patio slick and dangerous. The temperature seems to be dropping even more. The first guests open the patio door and slip and slide eagerly over to the bar table, and I crack the tops off a few bottled beers for them. A few want wine, and I use my trusty wine tool (I actually had one of those) to elegantly open some expensive Merlots. The minute they get their drinks, they run inside again to get away from the gradually worsening elements.

Then something unexpected happens. Night falls. This woman, who has obsessed about every detail in preparing for her party, who has carefully arranged bottles of liquor so they look attractive, who has fretted over the lengths of tablecloths, has forgotten that in the wintertime in New York it gets dark around five thirty. And she has no outdoor lights. So now the oyster guy and me are standing on an ice-slicked patio in freezing rain and complete blackness.

Every few minutes, the patio door opens and a few people come out for refills of drinks. They stand and shiver in the dark while my now-frozen hands claw at wine corks and beer caps.

"Aren't you freezing?" they all ask as they run back inside, not waiting for the obvious answer. I doubt any publishers or nymphomaniacs are going to want to chat with me under these conditions. But it could be worse. I could be the oyster-shucker kid. Nobody even visits his table. Waiting for him to shuck the oysters takes too long. He stands as close as he can to the steamer, shivering, shoveling oysters down his throat for warmth.

"Let me have an oyster or two," I say. He shucks them for me and eyes my table.

"Trade you," he says.

"What do you need?"

"A-a-anything," he says through chattering teeth.

I open a can of Coke, dump three quarters of it out, and pour some bourbon into the hole. "Try this." I like the idea and fix one for myself. I'm not sure it's legal to be serving alcohol to minors, but I'm also not sure it's legal to have them work in an ice storm. We are both bundled up like Eskimos now, and I realize that my nonreturnable cummerbund and bow tie cannot even be seen underneath my layers of survival gear.

Every few minutes, the door opens and someone rushes out and grabs a beer, asks us if we're freezing, and then runs back inside. Most of them are in such a hurry they don't even want to wait for me to make a drink. They just grab the first thing they feel on the table and dart off. So our being here is essentially pointless, except as a conversation piece: "And out the east window you'll see the two guys who are being paid to freeze in the dark. Or maybe you won't see them, but they're out there."

One of the wine bottles runs out and I have to open another, which is becoming difficult as I can no longer feel my fingers. When the wine drinkers have ducked back inside, the kid says, "Hey man, I think you cut yourself."

I look down. In the slivers of light coming through the blinds, I can see blood all over my hands, my coat, my wine tool. I must have stabbed myself earlier while opening a bottle of wine. I get a couple of wine glasses off the table and take them over to the window where there is enough light to check them. There is blood on every one. I check the beer bottles. Yup, blood.

I peer through the blinds at the party-goers, standing around in clusters next to the roaring fireplace, chatting away, with their blood-soaked wineglasses held at elegant angles, pinkies extended. At any second, I expect one of them to notice, and to hear a blood-curdling shriek of horror. Fortunately, most of them are drinking a nice, dark Merlot, so the color is almost indistinguishable.

"Come look at this," I tell the kid. He comes over. "They're drinking my blood."

He finds this funny. Way too funny. He bursts into shrieks of uncontrollable giggling and I realize he is plastered. When he catches his breath, he asks me, way louder than necessary and slurring slightly, if he can have another bourbon and Coke.

"Sure, why not."

Patrice sticks her head out the door. "You guys can break it down," she says. The kid thinks this is hilarious too. She looks at him oddly.

"Everything okay out here?" she asks me.

"Wonderful." Patrice seems a lot more upbeat now that her

party is going well, and she's had a few belts herself, but I don't know how she's going to feel about returning the kid to the neighbor's house covered in his own puke. There's still the issue of being paid to resolve, so it might be better if I just break down the oyster table for him.

"I'll take care of this," I tell him. All it involves is putting all the stuff in the garage. "Why don't you just go on home."

"Naw, I'm fine. I'm gonna go talk to Missy."

"Who's Missy?"

The kid explains that Patrice has a daughter to whom he has taken a shine, and he plans to go and introduce himself to her after his work here at the oyster table is finished.

"Why don't you let it go until tomorrow?" I advise. "I'm sure she's not going anywhere."

"MISSY!" he screams. He takes another swig of bourbon and Coke and staggers toward the house. I've created a fucking monster. He's going to go charging through the party like Ben Braddock from *The Graduate*, howling this girl's name. I intercept him and reason with him for a few minutes, and finally get him to start breaking the oyster table down, keeping a close eye on him. Fortunately, nature intervenes yet again, and a massive snowstorm begins. I now have an excuse to get the hell out of here.

I find Patrice in the kitchen, idly washing some wineglasses while she chats with a guest.

"Hi," I tell her. "It's snowing pretty bad out. I'd better be getting back into the city before they close the line."

"Sure," she says. She goes to get her purse. She pulls out cash. Stroke of luck. If it had been a check, I'd have had to go through the drawn-out process of telling her my name, revealing the dark secret that I wasn't Corey after she'd been calling me that all night. "Is Tony all right out there? He seemed odd."

"Cold was getting to him, I guess."

"It did get chilly, didn't it?" She hands me a wad of twenties. We say our good-byes. As I'm walking towards the door, I hear her guest who is holding a wineglass say, "Hey, is this blood?" I start walking faster. Outside, I look for Tony to say good-bye, and see that he is climbing up a drain pipe on the far wall of the house.

"Later, dude," I tell him.

"Shhhhh," he says. Then screams, "MISSY'S ROOM IS RIGHT HERE!"

"Yeah . . . well, have a good night." I run for the train station.

Cable, a God-given Right

Today is my birthday, and I get a nice surprise. I read a classified ad that says "English degree required." Those are three words you never see together, ever. It's like seeing "Must be a convicted criminal" or "Double amputees wanted." It just makes you wonder what the hell goes on at the place that ran the ad. This ad goes on to describe a need for someone a lot like me. "Retired colonel looking for full-time help running his new marketing firm. Must have good people skills, English degree required. Ex-military preferred."

I reach for the phone, imagining how thrilled the old colonel will be to hear from me. Ex-military, English degree, hell, I've got it all. The phone is answered by a stressed-out teenager who has obviously been fielding a flood of calls all day. There are more out-of-work, English-degree-bearing, ex-military types out there than I first thought, and I first thought there were plenty.

"Can I have your name, please" she asks in a monotone.

I tell her. "I'm calling about the ad."

"Be here tomorrow at nine thirty. Dress professionally."

"Where's here?"

This exasperates her, but she struggles through the anguish of providing me with the address. I can hear phones ringing in the background, and she is obviously in a hurry to get rid of me and be rude to someone new.

"I'll find it," I offer helpfully, letting her know that my military skill at map reading will enable me to find the address with no further assistance, but the phone is dead.

The place is a disused warehouse somewhere in Chelsea. I am greeted at the door by a hyperactive young man in a suit and tie who makes sincere eye contact with me as he scans a clipboard for my name. He is like the bouncer at an elite nightclub, making sure only to admit people who have made it through the demanding screening process, which consists of telling them your name. Or not even. Another youngish man, also nicely dressed, walks up behind me and says to the bouncer, "I heard about you guys," and is waved in.

I mill around in the lobby for a minute, examining the crowd, wondering if I have time to squeeze off one last cigarette before the fun begins. These are my people, the English degree owners, a faraway look in their eyes—the thousand-yard stare of a hundred tedious, underpaying jobs. Yet, I notice some groups are abuzz with positive energy. Off to my right, two women are talking excitedly about "a great opportunity." One woman, pretty and well-dressed, shakes my hand and introduces herself. Something is wrong. Women never talk to me first unless they're hookers or they need something heavy lifted.

My suspicions deepen. We sit down in folding metal chairs,

about thirty of us, and the young man who was checking people in comes up and asks us how we are doing. A few people
shout enthusiastically.

"Who here wants to make more money?" he asks.

The same people shout that they do.

"WHO HERE WANTS TO MAKE MORE MONEY?" He is
screaming with enthusiasm now, waving his arms like a quar-
terback trying to get more crowd noise. I am in the wrong
place. I meant to come to a job interview, not a Baptist revival.
Where's the kindly old colonel?

"What do you do for a living?" he asks one girl, a sweet-
looking twenty-something who seems to be uncomfortable in
her professional attire.

"I work in a coffee shop."

"Does that give you the financial freedom you need?"

"No way," she says. She is ready to be saved. The lady sitting
next to her is the one who introduced herself to me, and she
gently touches the younger girl's arm, nods at her, smiling.
Ohmygod, they've stocked the audience. This is a sales seminar,
and they've put salespeople in the audience to make the meeting go smoothly, like B-girls in a New Orleans dive bar. You
can't tell the customers from the employees.

I make a sport of it. I look around, trying to figure who's
who, and it's too easy. The people who look uncomfortable in
their own skin are the customers, the ad-respondents, and they
are seated every third person. I look to my left. A kindly older
gentleman nods at me enthusiastically. I look to my right. A
young man with thinning hair and glasses nods at me enthusiastically. It is masterful. This way, if any cynical or negative
comment occurs to me that I feel compelled to share with my
neighbor, he will quickly respond to it with corporate blather. It
is the sales version of a gang rape.

Each woman has two women on either side of her, each man

has two men. Some kind of corporate rule, I figure. That was why they bothered to ask us our names, to figure how many men and women they'd need to snow us. It must be a part of a salesperson's job to go to these meetings posing as an ad-respondent, bubbling with energy. If there are thirty people here and each ad-respondent has a salesperson on each side, that means there are only . . . let me see . . . not very many actual respondents.

"Here's Mike," says the bouncer, and claps. Everybody claps loud and long, and I get the feeling I should know who Mike is. I clap too. There's something contagious about applause.

Mike is a guy who has made a million dollars selling water filters. He doesn't actually mention a million dollars, but he speaks of having achieved "financial freedom." He breaks out a slide projector and shows us a slide of him standing in front of two Rolls Royces, wearing a Rolex. There is a really nice house in the background. For all I know, Mike might have broken on to the property with a photographer and posed for a few pictures before the owners released the Dobermans. But Mike is a well-dressed and imposing fellow, and he sure does look happy about water filters.

Mike walks over to a tap and pours some tap water into a beaker, then screws on a water filter and pours some more into a different beaker. He takes a syringe full of clear liquid and squeezes two drops of whatever is in the syringe into each beaker. The tap water turns purple. The filter water stays clear.

"THIS IS WHAT YOUR CHILDREN ARE DRINKING!" he thunders. You can't get much more scientific than that. I'm convinced. I don't have kids, but if I did, I wouldn't want them drinking purple water.

"Do you know what Evian is backwards?"

"Naïve!" a young man cries from the front row.

"That's right, *naïve*!" exults Mike. "Because that's what you have to be to pay a dollar for a quart of bottled water! These filters cost only forty dollars, and you can GET TEN THOUSAND GALLONS OF THE SAME QUALITY WATER AT ONLY TWO AND A HALF CENTS A GALLON!"

He's getting much too excited about this. I start shifting uncomfortably in my chair. But I notice one or two of the other real respondents are catching the fever.

"That's incredible!" one says. I wonder if he is a real respondent, or another plant. Maybe I'm the only one here; this is all for my benefit. Maybe I'll come back here tomorrow and this place will be an empty crackhouse, like a scene from *The Sting*, Maybe there's a camera trained on me, and guys up in a booth with headsets and microphones saying, "Bring it down a notch, Mike, we're losing him."

We watch a video, in which half a dozen ordinary people describe working in shitty jobs until they discovered the exciting world of water filter sales. "Now I have time to spend with my kids," one mother exults, and they show a full two minutes of her doing exactly that. All right, I get the picture. You've got kids and free time. A young man is shown in front of a pool, sipping a martini. "And I owe it all to the Dealmakers," he says. A bikini clad babe comes up and puts her arm around him, just in case the video had failed to engage the horny-man demographic. Fadeout.

The Dealmakers, as this marketing firm is called, then spend half an hour explaining how I can achieve financial freedom: by selling water filters to everyone I know. The thing is, everyone I know is like me. If we've got forty extra dollars lying around, it goes for a bag of weed or a one-night drinking binge, not to prevent some paranoid fantasy about purple water.

But Mike knows I'm thinking this. "You need to get your

friends and family healthy," he implores us. "They have no idea what they might be drinking." Then, he comes to the crux of the matter.

Mike acknowledges that some of us might not be professional salespeople, and that, initially, we're going to need some help. For a cool $500, he can set us up in a seminar with a man even more energetic and enthusiastic than himself. This man, whose name is spoken with reverence, only gives these seminars every six months because his time is in such demand, but it just so happens HE'S IN TOWN RIGHT NOW! We need to scrape together the money, we just must, or we'll be missing out on the greatest opportunity ever to come our way.

Five hundred dollars, Mike tells us, is barely half of what we'll make in our first week. People after my money always have an interesting way of describing it, as if my money was just a pain in my ass. Nobody who wants you to buy something from them reminds you how many days you had to get up early and drag your ass into work, how much humiliation you had to endure from abusive bosses and the eternally irritated public, just so you could earn that money. To them, it is stretching the leather on your wallet. That money is "doing nothing." Money should be used to earn money, they'll tell you. Even if you don't have a job. Especially if you don't have a job. Only dullards save their money for rent. Dreamers invest in WATER FILTER SALES!!!

The meeting breaks up, and the young man with thinning hair on my left is beaming. "Wow," he says. "What did you think of that?"

"It was great," I tell him, mimicking his enthusiasm. "I'm going to step outside and have a quick cigarette." As I am walking to the door, he starts to follow me, so I turn and say, "You know what, I have to take a shit first." He backs away.

As I'm walking to the bathroom, I see the coffee shop girl,

flanked on both sides by two pretty, well-dressed women who are beaming at her. She is beaming back. As I walk past, I hear her say, "I'm sure I can scrape up the money . . ."

There is an exit by the men's room that leads out to an alley. I step outside, light the cigarette, and tear off down the street.

There's no colonel. There's no need for military experience, nor an English degree. But if you advertise for people who have English degrees, you're reaching a great demographic: people who are frustrated and gullible, with a proven track record for poor decision-making. The trillion-dollar-industry-that-produces-nothing called "the educational system" got us, so we can be got again.

The next day, I get a phone call from the Dealmakers.

"Iain, we missed you yesterday after the meeting. Wanted to know if we could set you up with a pass for the seminar."

"Actually, I got another job already."

"Really? Doing what?"

"Stuffing ravioli."

"Is that going to give you the financial freedom you need?"

I hang up. I've had enough of this, the reading of stock phrases, the audience plants, the little marketing tricks awaiting me at every twist and turn. Why can't they leave me in peace? I'm not rich, the coffee shop girl wasn't rich. But who else is desperate enough to answer ads for fake opportunities? EARN THOUSANDS A WEEK AT HOME! BE YOUR OWN BOSS!!! I once answered an ad that said for fifty dollars I could get a list of companies in MY AREA who would hire me to work at home with a computer. They sent me a copy of the local yellow pages on a disk.

If I could sell even one water filter for them before I gave up in frustration, it would have been worth their while. Ten people a meeting, eight meetings a day, five days a week, that's four hundred water filters sold and $20,000 in seminar cash a week. And four hundred broke, tired slobs who've learned one more life lesson on their way to the grave.

I get a job driving an oil truck.

The pay is eight dollars an hour, but that's okay, because after I fill the oil truck with heating oil in the morning, I don't have to see a supervisor again until I hand him my receipts at the end of the day. I have a two-way radio in the truck, and they can call me from time to time and ask where I am, find out if I'm keeping to my schedule. But that's okay too, the schedule isn't that demanding.

The hard part is learning the route. I'm working Philadelphia's Main Line, once again servicing rich people, many of whom have mansions for houses. Families of three or four live in eighteen-bedroom castles, with new sports cars in every driveway. I drive around and wonder what these people do for a living. Where do the rich come from? Do all these houses belong to geniuses, inventors of rocket engines and cures for diseases? Did they have one great idea, like Post-it notes, and capitalize on it? Is there some fascinating story behind this great surplus of money, or have they simply inherited a factory that makes toenail clippers for the armed forces?

One thing's for sure; they believe they deserve it. I don't know many rich people, but I've met enough to know that even the ones who were handed a trust fund think of themselves as special, not lucky. They reinvent the past to include details of their own forbearance and fortitude to anyone who'll listen, and someone always will because they're rich. It's always more entertaining listening to the rich, because there's always a chance you'll be asked along to the Bahamas or given a sports car for the weekend. The fact that they're usually stingier than the people I hang out with takes a while to sink in.

The other great fact about rich people is that their kids are always fuck-ups. Not the kind of lovable fuck-up who works down at the gas station and tells you he can fix your car and then destroys it. No, rich kids are shady. They're the kind that dream up a brilliant illegal plan, just to show their dad a thing or two; then when you all get caught, they beg their dad for a great lawyer and never talk to you again. They were born into money, and they know money will take care of them. This security gives them a whole different value system, one the rest of the world never quite gets.

These half-empty houses, I notice, are mostly dark and quiet, like the set from *Citizen Kane*. Housewives putter around in the kitchens, and I see their coiffed heads through the window as I hook up my hose to their oil fills. They are usually alone. They never wave. The third great fact about rich people is that they don't talk to the help. *Lady Chatterley's Lover* was bullshit.

The hardest part is learning where the oil fill for each house is located. Each delivery notice provides a little map, but the fill itself is a metal pipe about five inches in diameter, and they are often behind bushes, under rocks, or buried completely in the snow. Sometimes the little fill maps are wrong altogether, and I spend fifteen minutes digging around in a prickly, snow-filled bush before noticing it on the far wall of the house, while the bemused housewife peers through her kitchen window wondering what I'm up to. Sometimes the driveway is configured so that I can't get the truck within a hundred yards of the oil fill, so I have to pull the hose across the front yard. Sometimes the hose feels like it's made of lead bricks. Sometimes the hose knocks over expensive lawn ornaments and I watch them shatter all over a cobblestone driveway. Sometimes the fill map is wrong because I'm delivering to the house next door, and I give them a hundred free gallons of heating oil before I realize this.

Instead of a map, one house has a delivery slip that says simply, "Fill at the donkey's nose." I pull up the driveway and notice a huge statue of a donkey in the front yard, so I go over and examine its nose. The donkey must be a heating oil tank, I decide. Its cement nostrils are large enough to accommodate an oil hose, though I don't see any threading in which to screw the gun. I jam the gun up its nostrils as far as it will go and turn on the oil full blast.

Immediately, the donkey's head explodes and I am showered with home heating oil and concrete. I grope around blindly for the hose, which is whipping around like an epileptic anaconda, spraying diesel fuel across this neatly landscaped yard. After taking a seventy-five-gallon-a-minute blast in the face at least three times, I manage to wrestle the hose to the ground and shut it off, having swallowed about a cupful of fuel. Choking and soaked, I limp back to the truck and call them on the radio.

"Yeah, I'm at 1105 Chester Springs. Their heating tank just broke."

"What do you mean it broke?" Charlie, the dispatcher, has been a deliveryman for fifteen years. He knows every delivery by heart.

"It just blew up all over me."

"That's the one beside the donkey, right?"

Beside the donkey? What did that mean? "Yes," I say cautiously.

"I'll get someone out there."

I put the radio back and run over to the headless, oil-soaked donkey. I scrape madly at the ground underneath the donkey's nose, and my hand hits metal under the snow. I sweep the snow aside, and there, laughing at me, is the oil fill.

"Fill is a noun and a verb," I explain. "Fill at the donkey's nose is ambiguous." I am sitting in Charlie's office, but he wants to get me out of there. Everyone wants me out, because I am soaked in heating oil and making them gag.

Charlie has been around a bit. He's not going to fire me because he's seen things like this before, and also because I am not the stupidest employee he has working for him today. That honor goes to another new guy named Dave, who filled a five hundred gallon septic tank with oil until diesel fuel sprayed out of the toilets and all over the bathrooms of a million dollar house in Kimberton. Then, while backing out of their driveway, he slammed into a pole and knocked their electricity out. So now these mansion dwellers are living in an oil-soaked cave, and Charlie has bigger things on his plate than a headless donkey.

"Get out of here," he tells me. "See you tomorrow at eight."

When the oil is pumping in, you hear a whistling sound, the air being released through a small vent as the tank fills up with oil. When the whistling stops, the tank is nearly full, and you shut the gun off. The problem is, I soon learn, that mice often crawl into the vent holes, which prevents the air from escaping. What happens then depends on how fat the mouse is. If you've got a nice thin mouse, he'll pop out and run off when the air starts pushing him out of the hole. A mid-sized mouse might make you think the tank is already full because you never get a good whistle and he's half stuck in the air tube, so you don't make the delivery. A nice fat mouse will stay in there, jammed, until the air pressure builds up enough to fire him out like a bullet.

After being shot with two mice on consecutive deliveries, I decide it's a good idea not to lean over the air holes. But this makes it hard to hear when the tank is filling up, and if you miss the gurgling sound that indicates fullness, oil comes spraying out of the vent. Often this doesn't matter, if it's a small quantity and the ground is just dirt. But when you get seven or eight gallons squirting into someone's prize-winning rosebushes, there's a problem.

About two nights a week I go home soaked in oil. One night, I do my laundry all together, work clothes and regular clothes mixed, and now I have an entire wardrobe that smells like diesel fuel. I have a girl over and she asks, "Is there a truck with a leak in the garage downstairs?"

The repairmen who have to keep answering spill calls are getting exasperated with me. Even Charlie is starting to take my mistakes a little more seriously. He asks me to work Christmas and New Year's Day, and I say yes, worried that refusal will send me back to another water filter meeting. I spend Christmas determined to be cheerful to everyone. I wave through the windows to the families inside, but nobody waves back. New Year's, I deliver oil all day with a raging hangover.

Then something happens. I get the hang of it. One day in February, Charlie is handing me my paycheck and he says, "You know what? You haven't had a spill call in a while." It's true, I realize. I've mastered oil delivery. The next time he hands me my paycheck, he tells me he's going to let me go.

"It's warm out," he says. "Business is dropping off to nothing. I only need one driver for all our routes."

I nod.

"Seasonal work, you know how it is. You did a great job." He pats me on the shoulder.

Back to the classifieds.

I have a friend whose dad needs his garage painted, and I figure the money from that will help while I search for something else. While we're driving to get paint, he tells me about his life.

"I bought my first house for nine thousand dollars," he says. We are in a car that cost twice that. "It was a nice house too. Nowadays, you couldn't get a crackhouse for nine thousand."

He has worked most of his life selling air conditioners. That wouldn't bring in enough now to live in a one-bedroom apartment, even for a gifted salesman. Where has the money gone, and when did it go? Was it the Trilateral Commission, the Gang of Seven? Reaganite defense contractors, yuppies, the Japanese? Is that the money they're talking about when they discuss the National Debt? Was that four trillion dollars the money that would have gotten me paid enough to live in a cheap house? How did the National Debt occur? How do I get my share back?

Everybody has a different theory. He's decided it's Reaganite defense contractors. That sounds about right to me. I don't know enough about it to argue.

Someone took all the money, that's for sure. It's got to be around somewhere, there was so much of it. Maybe it was the trickle-down theory of economics in reverse, the trickle-up theory. It just slowly bled away from the American people, as one careless decision after another allowed the millionaires to carve off a bigger piece every day. The wealthy philanthropists, the Andrew Carnegies of yesteryear who lamented the plight of the poor, have been replaced by a new breed of millionaire, the rich born-millionaire who doesn't know that poverty exists. It's every millionaire for himself.

One factory moved to Mexico today, one pay raise for Congress tomorrow, one government official turning a blind eye to the phone companies raising their rates the day after that, and pretty soon, everybody's scraping by. The home builders see an opportunity to jack up the prices, and no one tells them no. Where was the guy who was supposed to say, "No, that wouldn't be fair"? Was there ever such a guy? Did the authors of the Constitution neglect to include a paragraph on what should happen when wealth started to separate from the people into the hands of an elite few?

If you ask the rich why you're not capable of supporting yourself, they'll tell you it is your fault. The ones who make it to the lifeboats always think the ones still in the water are to blame. Weren't quick enough, sharp enough, weren't on the ball. Didn't see the economic shipwreck in time. Should've invested in computers. Should've started learning about computers when you were eight. Should've taken computer classes instead of baseball elective in seventh period, then you'd be where I am now.

I pour the paint into the pan and get to work.

It's easy enough. Too easy, actually, and the line between working and accepting charity quickly begins to blur. I work for about two hours and my friend's dad asks me if I want a dip in the pool. I try to stay businesslike and tell him I have to work. He shrugs. It's all the same to him. I'm his son's friend, and I'm getting paid whether I go swimming or finish the garage. I try to do an excellent job, but there's no real challenge, and upon completion there's nothing to appreciate. The garage has a new coat of paint. It'll last a few more years.

Later in the day, after returning home, a neighbor asks me if I know anything about cable television. I'm handy enough, and I figure his cable has gone out, so I offer to have a look.

"I'm trying to get hooked up," he tells me.

"Ah-hah." He is looking at me with the apprehensive glance I'm familiar with, the questioning look to determine whether you are in the brotherhood. I am.

A few years ago, I worked for a tree service, and the owner, while trying to teach me how not to electrocute myself, was kind enough to give me an unwitting lesson in cable theft. He was a hardworking, honest man who had spent his whole life working up around telephone, cable, and electric wires, and he carefully explained to me the nature of each. It takes me about five minutes to get my neighbor a connection, and he slips me fifty bucks.

The next day, one of his friends calls. Then another. Then friends of theirs call. Everyone is clamoring for free cable. One guy actually has his legit cable shut off and then calls. Apparently, I have become the unofficial cable installer in my neighborhood. I'm over at a girl's house getting drunk one night, and she is lamenting the poor quality of network television, and the next thing she knows, she has cable. My friend wants to watch a sporting event that is being filtered out with his cable package, so I unscrew a filter and we settle down for an evening's entertainment.

Contrary to what the ads would have you believe, stealing cable is an act of civil disobedience which would make Martin Luther King and Mahatma Gandhi proud. The word "pirates" is often ascribed to cable thieves, a word used by the media, most of which are owned by the same people who own the cable networks. They try to convince us that cable thieves are eroding American morality. Closing profitable factories, laying off hundreds of workers and reopening the factories in Mexico with cheaper labor is not indicative of an erosion of morality. Paying mushroom pickers four dollars an hour is not illegal. Watching *Pop-up Video* for free, now that's a crime.

This is my rationale for stealing cable. My term for people who steal cable would be "Robin Hoods." I'm standing in line here at the Time-Warner office in Durham, North Carolina, with a girl who has come to pay her cable bill. We are behind a young black couple who are begging to have their cable reinstalled, even though they have fallen behind in their payments. The girl behind the window is as heartless as any of the Sheriff of Nottingham's men.

"You need to make good on the $63.95, then we'll send someone out. And there'll be a $23.95 reinstallation charge."

The woman starts to protest and the girl cuts her off. "I gotta have the money. Rules are rules."

Rules are indeed rules, but the people who make them are often mad with greed. And cable is a God-given right of every American, something to which we should all be entitled. The premium channels are for the rich, TNT and USA for the rest of us. But NO cable at all? Come on, have a heart.

Back when I was in high school, nobody had cable, everybody watched network TV. Now every house on every street pays an average of eighteen dollars a month to watch *History of the World, Part One* seven times a month. This is millions upon millions of dollars flowing into someone's bank account. Where do these millions go? They sure as hell don't go to programming. I get twenty-four-hour-a-day free cable, and that means episodes of *Columbo* and *Hawaii Five-O*, which I didn't think were good even when I was a kid. Cable has taken our money and recycled yesterday's garbage and fed it back to us.

So what's the harm in planting a splitter, or acquiring a descrambler box? With a descrambler you can watch the late night porn channels and look at some silicone-breasted nymph sprawl around on a bed without paying eight dollars for the privilege. Who has the patience for more than five minutes of that anyway? By the time I've heard her tell me she likes swimming in the sea and doesn't like rude people, I've usually been ready for more of Steve McGarrett catching the one-dimensional killer du jour. If Time-Warner wanted twelve dollars a month, they'd get it. If they want the equivalent of a car payment, they'll get nothing and like it.

The tragedy of a career in cable theft, however, is that unlike some criminal ventures, such as drug-dealing and prostitution, cable theft has no repeat customers. Soon, the well is dry. Everyone in my neighborhood is snuggled up watching Comedy Central and Nickelodeon, and I have to reenter the work force.

I get a job cooking in a restaurant.

Wouldn't We All Be Happier Somewhere Else?

The irony of the restaurant industry is that no restaurants ever open up in areas of high unemployment, the logic being that these areas are economically depressed and the local populace doesn't have the disposable income to spend on luxuries like eating out. This means that anywhere there are people who really need restaurant jobs, the restaurants are fleeing like crazy, only to open in areas where nobody wants to work in them. The result is that every successful restaurant is staffed solely with employees who would rather be somewhere else.

While this might be true of most businesses, restaurant people don't make any bones about it. "I'm getting a real job next week," one of the waitresses tells me on my first day. "As soon as I graduate, I'm getting a real job," the cook who trains me says. There's an unspoken understanding among the employees that their jobs are not real, partly because they were so easy to get and partly because restaurant work doesn't command respect. So employees are always on the lookout for something better, no matter how much money they're making.

Restaurants combat this the same way most corporations combat eroding morale: by offering meaningless job titles and fake benefits. But in the restaurant industry, eroding morale is a given, so they don't waste too much time with it. "We offer full medical after ninety days," the bleary-eyed manager tells me during my orientation. Then he adds, "And our home office deducts the expense from your paycheck." He makes it sound like the home office staff is doing me a favor, saving me the trouble of subtracting my own money from my check. I check the "Insurance declined" space on the form.

"You also qualify to be a shift leader after ninety days," he tells me, and I would decline that too, if there was an option. Shift leaders are the corporate restaurant world's answer to prison trustees. For an extra fifty cents an hour, you become responsible for everything, basically performing management functions for cook's pay. This frees the managers up to do the more important things, like wander around and look stressed, or sit at a table and wait for the night to end so they can start in on the hard liquor when there's no one around.

"Let's get to work," he tells me.

The restaurant is one of those springing up everywhere, the defining characteristic being crap nailed to the walls. Sometime in the early eighties, someone somewhere decided that people felt more comfortable eating with a refinished canoe paddle nailed to the wall behind them. Busted brass lamps and blacksmith's tools soon followed, and now every corporate restaurant in the United States sports a wealth of garage sale refuse secured to the walls; secured very well, I might add, so drunk people can't pry it off.

The food in these places is bland but palatable, and the restaurant where I have just been hired is no exception. There is a page in the handbook for every step of every process in the preparation of every menu item. It isn't cooking that I'm doing here as much as production. I'm essentially a factory worker. One of the managers is a cooking school grad who was fired up with new ideas when he was hired six months ago, and has now resigned himself to slapping burgers into molds with a look of disgust. "I'm going to get a real job," he tells me as he shows me how to use the burger mold. "I've applied at Payne Walker."

"Isn't that a slaughterhouse?"

"It's meat cutting. You get to use a skill."

I've worked in actual factories, and the workers are happier than the people here. The people here are not allowed to admit that they are involved in a production line, and the managers are in charge of the collective denial. We read weekly bulletins sent to us from corporate headquarters that tell us how well we are doing, how we are pleasing "guests" (the new word for customers), how we must keep smiling, even in the kitchen where the guests can't see us. Scowls are picked up by the waitstaff, who then scowl at the guests, who leave and don't come back; and then the restaurant is closed and we're all looking for jobs. So if we like being employed, we'd better smile. That's the logic.

It looks good on paper, but the philosophy fails to take into account the complexity and perversity of human nature. Directives to grin have the opposite effect on me. Smiles come from somewhere else. The end result is waitstaff and floor personnel gripped with a forced neurotic enthusiasm, which they substitute for actual pleasantness. This manifests itself in unnecessarily loud speech, so everyone walks around and screams at each other, and the guests.

"HOW ARE YOU TODAY, DAVID?" a perky female manager asks me at the beginning of my second day. Enthusiasm comes from the top, so the managers have to be the perkiest of us all.

"My name's Iain," I tell her quietly.

She pumps me on the shoulder and wanders off. Later in the day, after a busy lunch shift, she comes back behind the cook line and looks at us, clearly worried.

"WHAT'S THE MATTER WITH YOU GUYS?" she asks. The other cook, an older Nigerian named Jacques who has worked here for years, stares at her. I'm trying to learn a new menu and to get the ingredients right in a salad I'm making.

"We busy," says Jacques. I nod in agreement.

"EVERYBODY'S BUSY," she yells. "COME ON, KICK IT IN GEAR!"

I'm convinced this is just silliness, and I'll get used to it, and I spend the next few days making an effort to learn the menu and get things right. The work is hard, but Jacques is a good teacher and easy to work with. I mind my own business, show up on time, and do everything the handbook tells me is required. At the end of the week, the manager, Marci, calls me into the office for "counseling."

"You don't seem happy here," she tells me. She isn't screaming now. She's looking at me intensely, as if daring me to say the wrong thing, and a hundred wrong things occur to me. What's happiness got to do with it? That would be wrong. Fuck you. That would be wrong too.

"I'm fine," I say.

"You don't seem fine."

What am I supposed to say to that? I'm here. I was on time and sober. What do they want? I stare at her, convinced if I say anything, it'll come out wrong.

"What do you have to say?"

"Nothing, really."

"Would you be happier somewhere else?"

"No," I lie. Wouldn't we all be happier somewhere else? Isn't that a mainstay of the human condition? I don't think it was a philosophical question.

She shrugs her shoulders and throws up her hands, as if to say, "What am I going to do with you?" Something else is going on here, I figure, as it always is. I've done a fine job, I'm an experienced and reliable cook, but they always want something more than just what the classified ad tells you. They want a good ass-kissing. I might be capable of it, if it wasn't demanded from me.

"I'll give you another week," she tells me as she turns away, ending the meeting. I leave quietly.

"What was that about?" Jacques asks.

"She thinks I have a bad attitude."

Jacques laughs. "She not been fucked in a year."

A week goes by, and Marci never talks to me again. My attitude is no different, but the restaurant is so understaffed that even she has the common sense not to fire me just to prove she can. Restaurants are sprouting up in the area like weeds. Fourteen corporate restaurants have opened in the past six months, and with each one needing about sixty employees, that's 840 people who can get jobs. Restaurants fight aggressively for staff, offering bounties to employees who bring in friends, running larger and larger newspaper ads, even offering sign-on bonuses. It's an employee's market, and I'm riding the wave.

The work is hard, but the people I work with are hard

workers. All of them have another job, and many go straight from one job to the other five or six days a week. This makes for a seventy-hour work week with no overtime, having to be on your feet the whole time. They never complain. The common refrain is, "You get used to it."

I've worked seventy-hour weeks, often for months on end, but I'd never say I got used to it. My body was fighting for rest the whole time. But if you want your own apartment, or an insured car, or legal cable, it's now a necessity. What single job can provide one individual with a comfortable lifestyle? So by the time these guys have paid for all the things they want, they never have time to use them because they're always at one restaurant or another, throwing burgers on a grill.

I prefer to keep my time off and just get by.

Robb, the manager who dreams of one day working in a slaughterhouse, is intrigued by the fact that I have a college degree. "You could go into management with that," he tells me. "You're underutilized."

"What's so great about management?"

"More money, for starters. Look at you. You're wasting yourself."

I hear that a lot, but the options aren't all that intriguing. In order to not waste myself, I have to have a career in management and work a minimum of sixty hours a week doing essentially the same things I'm doing now. If you factor in twenty hours of overtime, it doesn't pay more, it just offers more work. In fact, it pays about a dollar an hour less.

"You'd get benefits," he adds excitedly. "And sick days."

This is a man who desperately wants to get rid of his job and is trying to convince me how attractive it is. "You don't like your job," I point out.

"It's not for me. But it'd be perfect for you."

Is he trying to groom me to replace him? He's a straightforward fellow, not one to have a hidden agenda. I think he just wants the best for me.

"I'll think about it," I say, and he rolls his eyes at my stubbornness. I'm taking home over $300 a week here, no stress. When I'm done, I go. There's no possibility of them transferring me to another store, like they do with managers. Most importantly, I can mind my own business, and don't have to wander around making sure everyone is grinning.

The next week, Ken, the general manager, stops me as I'm punching out to go home. "I hear you're interested in management," he says.

"Not really." I don't relish the extra work, but there's a security in management, the idea that you're working toward some kind of career goal, a hope of advancement. These are things that I've been thinking about as I get older. As a manager, you're under some kind of umbrella, protected.

"We're looking for managers," he tells me. "Why don't I give you the module book and let you look it over."

I take the module book, the manager's training manual, which has the whole sixty-day process outlined in extreme detail. I already know the kitchen, which is the hardest part. As part of the training, I also have to bartend and host, and wait tables for a shift or two, all things I have done before. It seems easy enough, but I'm not sure I want to deal with the hours required.

Then the area director comes in to see me one afternoon as I am closing down the line for a lunch shift. He shakes my hand and smiles heartily.

"I hear you're going to be one of our new managers," he says.

These people must be desperate. I've never really expressed a desire to anyone, yet word is traveling up the chain that I'm driven and ambitious, looking to climb the corporate ladder, all because I failed to say no to the prospect of a promotion. It's too late to back out now, so I do what I usually do when questioned about jobs I don't really want. I ask for an impossible amount of money.

"Thirty-two thousand a year?" the area director says. He smiles. I smile. I know John is making twenty-six, and that this is probably out of the question. I'm making nine dollars an hour now, so he knows I can survive on a lot less. I figure he'll make me an insulting counteroffer and I can go back to cooking.

"I like your style," he says. "You're ambitious."

He's actually considering my request, mistaking my desire to end the conversation quickly for business savvy. He nods. "That isn't out of the question," he tells me.

It isn't? Damn. Now I'm going to have to make a decision. Turn my life upside down for a restaurant I haven't yet decided I like, or continue to live in poverty. Poverty has been going on too long.

"We'll get back to you," he says.

So two days later, I'm wearing a tie and wandering around doing nothing. Jeff, the area director, goes over the module book with me in great detail, explaining each step, what I am supposed to learn on each day. Then he leaves and the module book is thrown out by the other managers. They are desperately understaffed and they just want a warm body to pick up slack, so I am assigned a myriad of menial chores.

On day one, my manager training consists of cleaning the toilets and replacing air fresheners, then driving across town to pick up liquor. After that, I go back into the kitchen to make onion rings for seven hours because one of the prep cooks failed to show. On day two, the opening waitresses both fail to show, so I do all their opening side work, then make onion rings for seven hours. The kitchen manager, who is desperate to unload some responsibility, tries to get me to do the food order without explaining to me how to do it, and rather than see the restaurant run out of everything, I wind up having an argument with the guy. Then Marci, the closing night manager who only two weeks before was threatening to fire me, decides she doesn't feel safe closing alone because she has received a prank phone call during the day, and suspects robbers or rapists might come in after the restaurant has closed. My instinct is to tell her to take her chances, but I'm supposed to be professional now. I sit at the bar for three more hours, not drinking, but waiting, watching sports highlights over and over while Marci does paperwork. By the time I leave, I've been there thirteen hours.

I spend the better part of the next month mopping floors and making onion rings, working over seventy hours a week. I am now working thirty more hours a week and averaging, after taxes, ninety more dollars per paycheck. Furthermore, I have become a lightning rod for blame. The night cooks forget to change the fry oil one night, and we open with burned grease. Nobody has ordered fresh fry oil, so we have to spend the lunch shift serving blackened french fries. Jeff comes in and sees this.

"Did you see this fry oil?" he screams at me. The days of handshaking and smiles are over.

"Yes."

"What have you done about it?"

"We're getting a truck tomorrow."

"Goddamnit, we need fresh grease today. What are you going to do about it?"

I am fresh out of ideas. I'm supposed to be a trainee. People are supposed to be showing me what to do.

"We're not paying you this kind of money to just wander around," he tells me. "Call another restaurant and get them to lend us some grease."

This makes sense, and while I am doing it, he comes in and screams about the lettuce.

"We've got lettuce rotting in the back of the freezer! Why aren't you rotating it?"

"I've been making onion rings," I tell him.

"You're not supposed to be making onion rings. You're supposed to be managing. Get someone else to make the onion rings! I want you watching the lettuce and fry oil quality!" He storms off.

He's living in a dreamworld. We're fresh out of employees. He thinks we have prep cooks lined up dying to work. In reality, if we've got three prep shifts a week covered, I'm happy. I go back to making onion rings because we're almost out of them.

Jeff comes back into the kitchen a few hours later, sees me working at the stainless steel table. "Can I talk to you for a minute?"

"Is it about onion rings?"

"Let's just talk."

I know how the conversation is going to go. I take off my apron.

"I'll be in to pick up my paycheck," I say.

I walk home.

So that's how it goes. I should have just stuck with a nice nine-dollar-an-hour job, minding my own business. As soon as you start to move up, you're asking for trouble. There's nothing up there but ambitious, driven people trying to get you to do more of their work for less of their money.

For the rest of us, the dream has nothing to do with it. It's avoiding the nightmare that counts. I'm walking along a busy street peopled with the homeless and the nearly homeless, the walking, talking reminders of what happens when the bottom falls out. I have about ninety dollars left until my next payday, and after that, nothing. What divides me from them? Ninety dollars.

A guy comes up and asks me for some spare change. I wonder if he is doing better than me, financially. In Philadelphia, I remember working a Friday night at a restaurant where a homeless man would stand outside begging for change from our customers. At the end of the night, I had made sixty-five dollars, and he'd made seventy. How much money is there in begging? I've never tried it, maybe I should give it a whirl. You can pick your own hours and be your own boss. Isn't that the American dream? Maybe I should become an independent finance acquisition specialist.

This guy reeks of alcohol, and his skin is as leathery as a saddlebag. He is having trouble standing as he tries to focus. Maybe he isn't doing better than me, for now anyway. I give him two dollars and send him on his way.

I have a friend, Jim, from a restaurant job a long time ago, who was recently hired by a national moving company, and he has a job driving a tractor trailer across all fifty states. There is a message from him on my answering machine when I get home, telling me he needs help. How timely.

Jim wants to pay me $500 a week to drive and help load the truck. He's been having a problem lately because every time he pulls into a new city, the company he works for is supposed to provide laborers to help him move people's furniture onto the truck. Most of them are stoned, drunk, and useless, and they keep breaking the furniture, which he has to pay for.

First, I have to get a truck driver's learner's permit, which is easy enough. I go down to the DMV and take a short test. Now I can drive as long as he's in the cab. Then I arrange to have all my stuff put in storage. I say good-bye to my roommate, and catch a cheap early morning flight to Nashville, Tennessee, where I meet Jim at the airport.

"Damned good to see you," Jim says, shaking my hand. "It's nice to finally have someone you can trust out here." It's been about a year since I've seen him, but he looks a good deal older. He has bags under his eyes and has developed a nervous tic. The freewheeling drinker I knew from the restaurant has disappeared.

We go to dinner in downtown Nashville, and Jim describes his life since he was hired by the moving company seven weeks ago. He's been all over the country: Chicago, Las Vegas, Texas, Florida, and up the East Coast. He hasn't had either the time or the money to appreciate any of this, however, because he's spent the whole time either in a truck or in people's houses loading their furniture onto the truck. Every customer has a particular pick-up and drop-off date, which the company provides, and often the schedules are nearly impossible to meet. So someone might have a pick-up in Nashville tomorrow, but since there is a drop-off in Memphis the next day, nothing from the Nashville load can be put in front of the Memphis load, or it will all have to be unloaded again, taking hours. The truck has to be packed accordingly. He's learning this by experience. He tells me stories of one logistical disaster after another.

"I was in Las Vegas," he says, "and the company says the guy has nine thousand pounds. There was twelve thousand there easy. The company agents bid on jobs just to get them. They don't care about the truckers, they get paid according to how many jobs they get. So the agents always quote the customers a lower price than you'd expect. The thing is, I don't have room in my truck for the extra three thousand pounds."

"What'd you do?"

"I refused the shipment. You can refuse two a year. So I drive all the way to Las Vegas from Chicago for nothing. I'm an independent contractor, I have to pay for the gas."

"And the customer doesn't get moved?"

John shrugs. "Not by me. That's the agent's problem. He should learn to make quotes."

I imagine a guy who was all prepared to move, everything wrapped, in boxes, waiting for his truck, and when it shows, the driver sees how much stuff he has and drives off.

"You gotta stick up for yourself," Jim tells me. "Otherwise they'll eat you alive."

They'll eat you alive anyway.

The first day we have a pick-up in Nashville, a small one. A young woman getting married is moving from an apartment in Nashville to a house in Spokane, Washington. Then we hightail down to Huntsville, Alabama, where a young woman getting divorced is moving all her stuff into storage. Circle of life.

Between each move, we have to find a weigh station to weigh the truck, so we can find out how much each load is and charge the customer accordingly. The nearest weigh station in this case is nearly a hundred miles from the woman's storage space, so driving back and forth to the station in the pouring rain takes up most of the day. We get done at one in the morning. We sleep in a motel, which costs forty dollars.

At six we are up and cruising empty to Topeka, Kansas, which Jim hopes to reach by nightfall. The mileage directory says this is 758 miles away, and truckers are only allowed to drive ten hours a day. This means we'll either have to average 75.8 miles per hour, which is illegal, or drive more than ten hours, which is also illegal. Jim puts down in the logbook that we started at nine thirty, which creates problems of its own.

Now, if we get pulled over between six and nine thirty, Jim loses his license because he's driving without being logged. Furthermore, if we get pulled over at ten o'clock, and we're 250 miles out of Huntsville, we have to explain to a state trooper how we drove 250 miles in a half hour. So my job is to keep a fake logbook full of horseshit information that makes everything look okay.

I can't even begin to get the hang of it. I'm supposed to keep records of the truck mileage when we cross state lines, which is easy enough, but in the fake logbook the mileages have to be different. Then if we get pulled over and the trooper looks at the current mileage on the actual odometer and sees my written mileage, which we're not going to hit until some time tomorrow, we're screwed. There's no way to pass a thorough inspection.

"There's no way to do this and make it work," I tell Jim.

"Just try."

"Why don't we just pull into Topeka tomorrow afternoon?"

"The company promised we'd be there tomorrow morning."

The public likes a professional moving company. They also like having their stores stocked with everything they need. Then they like the idea that trucks driving on the road are regulated by some kind of governing body, making sure the vehicles are safe and the drivers aren't all falling asleep at the wheel. It's just not possible.

Everybody wants fresh vegetables, fresh fish, fresh coffee, fresh cut flowers. Warehouses are going out of style. Everything must be brought in that day. Consumer tastes are pushing the trucking industry to hurry up, while more and more cops are flooding the roads to make them slow down. Thousands of federal and state employees have created laws and devised a system, with logbook directives and weigh stations and checkpoints, and thousands of truckers are trying to outsmart it to make a living. The trucker who doesn't need to outsmart it either has a luxurious job or no bills to pay.

As darkness starts to fall, Jim tells me what I hope is an apocryphal story of the trucker who drove five minutes over ten hours, then got broadsided by a drunk driver in a car. The car driver's passenger died. The accident was deemed entirely the trucker's fault, because he was over his ten hour limit.

"So get the books right," Jim tells me.

My attempt at log-keeping wouldn't fool even the dumbest state trooper, but it turns out not to matter because we blow a trailer tire heading into Kansas. This slows us down enough to make everything legal, which is to say, backed up. I sit in the cab and madly erase everything I have written so far, then scribble in the real numbers. By the time I am done, the logbook looks like a mad scientist's chalkboard.

"We're going to have to spend the night here," says Jim, dejected. He has failed in his mission. He has not kept the schedule. I point out that the schedule is unrealistic and he stares at me as if I just don't understand. I don't. We drive the truck into a motel parking lot and Jim waits for the wrecker while I get us a room.

Another forty dollars. We decided that, as there are two of us, we'll sleep in the cramped sleeper only when there is no option. We are splitting the room cost, which is twenty dollars per person per night, $140 per week out of my five hundred. Then

there is food. We have to eat every meal at a diner, so I'm looking at twenty dollars a day minimum for food, which sucks up
another $140. By the time I get my money, it's chump change,
$220 for a seventy-hour week. With overtime, this averages out
to about $3.80 an hour.

Jim comes into the hotel room, devastated. He is carrying
logbooks and maps, and he sits at the little desk, feverishly
going over details. I am trying to watch *Law and Order*.

"Could you keep that down?" he asks, irritated. So I watch
Law and Order with the sound off, which takes away a lot of
the effect, as the show is mainly dialogue. Then, after about five
minutes he looks up and says, "We have to leave at five in the
morning."

"What for?" Now I'm pissed.

"So we can make our schedule."

"The people who made up the schedule are sitting in an
office in Beaumont, Texas. It was just an idea they came up
with. Why don't you just call them tomorrow and tell them
we're running late because we lost a tire."

"We have to keep to the schedule."

"Then call the customer and tell them we'll be late."

"The schedule says to be there at seven. We'll be there
at seven."

Damn if we're not there at seven.

"You can achieve it if you put your mind to it," Jim tells me,
guru-like, as we pull up at the house. He thinks I lack desire,
that burning in the gut that makes you want to accomplish
goals. I do. I think the goals are meaningless.

I get out of the truck, go inside the house, and look around.
It is a beautiful house, spotless white carpet, cathedral ceilings,
maple wood lining every windowsill and door frame. The furni-

ture is quality stuff too, all mahogany or cherry wood. The kitchen is the size of a restaurant's. But I notice something else.

People prepare for moves differently. In a good scenario, boxes are taped up and labeled, drawers emptied, televisions unplugged, beds stripped. In a bad scenario, which is what this is, it looks like it was your idea to show up and move them, that the truck in the driveway caught them by surprise. Televisions are still on, items like plants and ornaments are still everywhere, books are still in the bookcases, and the beds are made. Nothing has been done.

I open the fridge. It is full. I open the pantry door. It is full.

A pretty woman, about forty, wearing sweatpants and a T-shirt, comes inside and looks around sheepishly. "I got a lot done last night," she says.

I nod. A lot of what, I wonder? I had a mental picture of her packing a few things, then throwing the packing tape down when it started to occur to her how long this ordeal was going to go on, and mumbling to herself, "Let the movers do it." Let us pack, strip her beds, take down her pictures, unplug her TVs. Some people just don't have a taste for manual labor of any kind, especially not if there's the money to pay someone else to do it.

Packing is easy work, compared to moving, and there is so much extra stuff in the house that it will take us all day just to get organized enough to start loading the truck. Jim calls the company and gets her estimate adjusted, essentially charging this woman a thousand or so extra dollars for the inconvenience she has caused. She shrugs. It's just money to her, and the less she has to bother with the better.

I start wrapping her trinkets in paper, three or four sheets of thick moving paper around each figurine, an environmentalist's nightmare. Each 4.5-cubic-foot box can hold only a handful of the tiny, glass artifacts with which she has lined her whole house. This is the way it has to be done because as we are now charging her for packing, we are responsible for the breakage of anything that was packed. Even more time consuming is the inventory list. Every remote control, box of fish food, aquarium rock, and egg timer that we drop in a box has to be accounted for, to protect the lady from us stealing her stuff. Of course, as I am in charge of both inventory and packing, all I have to do if I want to steal something is just not inventory it, but this doesn't matter. Like most services that corporations offer, it's just a marketing trick, designed to make the customer feel good.

While Jim and I are working, the woman starts telling us the story of her life. She is moving out the day before her husband comes home from a business trip because she has recently discovered that he molested their daughter when she was a child. The daughter shared this with the woman after a particularly emotional therapy session, and the woman decided to schedule a move when he was away. So this man will be coming home from a business trip to an empty house, and later in the week he'll get served with all kinds of legal papers.

This seems like personal stuff to be telling a mover, but Jim and I just nod and continue about our business. She tells us more gory details about her life and dysfunctional marriage. She mentions that she was a farmer's daughter from one of the poorest areas in Kansas, and that she had met her husband while they were in college, where she had received a scholarship for winning a beauty contest. But, like a guilty party in a murder interrogation, she doesn't stop talking in time, and bits of information start to emerge to tell a different story.

It seems that her husband only recently brokered a deal to make him one of the richest men in town. This coincided nicely with the divorce proceedings, and the "sudden" realization of the molestation. Now that this man has something worth suing for half of, all the skeletons are suddenly coming out of the closet. This woman is clever, astute. She's been biding her time since she met this man in college for just this day, just this carefully planned opportunity. Now, thanks to Jim and myself, and this fine moving company, she can make herself the well-to-do matron she always must have wanted to be, ever since she looked at the rich women in town from the back of her daddy's pickup.

I guess that's one way to get out of a life of poverty. It makes us the getaway drivers in a heist.

We've been packing for ten hours before we can even start loading. It is pitch black before we can get to the heavy stuff, and we have to spend forty minutes rigging flashlights in the truck so we can see. By two in the morning we've stopped caring about any of her possessions, and so has she. We slam a lawn mower up against a TV set, balance a mirror on top of a big pile of garden rakes. We are running out of room in the truck, and we still have a pile of boxes and assorted junk from the garage to go. A few of the boxes get crammed in so tightly they lose their shape, and I hear the occasional tinkling of broken glass from inside. We stuff what we can into the belly box, the metal bin on the underside of the trailer designed to carry the moving ramps. The last few boxes go into the sleeper, along with a pile of rope and some small lamps and garden tools.

At three thirty in the morning we finish. She signs the paperwork, waves good-bye, and shuts the door. No tip.

We've just worked a twenty-hour day on five hours' sleep. According to our schedule, we should be in Colorado by now, on our way to Spokane. Even Jim is beginning to admit that the war is unwinnable.

"I don't think I can keep on like this without any real rest," he tells me, his eyes red-rimmed, like my own. Unlike me, he has an hour of paperwork to take care of before he can drift off to sleep in the first motel we find that takes trucks. "Let's just spend a day in Boulder, relax."

"Sounds good."

"Fuck 'em, I don't care what they say," he tells me anxiously, meaning the people in the office.

"It's not a do-able schedule."

"They're killing me."

"I know."

We blow another tire.

Fortunately, there is a rest stop about a mile ahead, and we limp into it.

We are both too tired to curse or complain, and all we want is sleep. This is impossible because the sleeper is crammed full of boxes, lamps, and rakes. I try to make enough room in the sleeper to lie down by shoving everything into the passenger seat, and the bottom falls out of one of the boxes, dumping this lady's memorabilia all over the cab. We look at each other, an unspoken agreement to worry about it tomorrow. I push and kick a few more boxes out of the way, and have enough room for a halfway comfortable lying position.

Jim, who is considerably shorter than me, manages to rig up a board across the cab and lie down there. A rake, which has been jammed into place by the boxes I have just kicked, is pointing straight into his back. Irritated, he rolls under the rake and kicks it up with his foot, splintering into a dozen pieces. Then he grabs the pieces, opens the door, and throws them into the rest area parking lot.

When he slams the door shut, I am convulsing with laughter.

"What's so funny."

I am laughing so hard I can hardly breathe or speak. "You . . . just . . . broke . . . that lady's rake." After spending fifteen hours trying so hard to treat her stuff carefully and professionally, after double and triple wrapping every trinket and figurine she owned, we are kicking and slamming and destroying anything that inconveniences us.

Jim starts giggling too.

"Let's just hope she doesn't pull into this rest stop."

I sleep very well, and in the morning I get up and realize that the things I spilled all over the cab are modeling photographs. We have ten- and fifteen-year-old shots of her in a bikini, in ski wear, modeling lingerie, even a few nudes. We ooh and ahh over them while we drink coffee from a rest stop vending machine and wait for the repair truck.

"She was a good looking woman," Jim says, admiring the photos from several different angles.

"Still is."

"Fucked her way into some serious money."

"God bless her. I would if I could."

"Would you?"

I give this some thought. It's a purely theoretical question. I've never met a rich woman who I've gotten along with well enough to get such an offer. Probably not, I decide. "I reckon if I would, I'd have probably done it by now."

"Yeah," Jim says, putting the photos down. "I could live off a rich girl for a few weeks, but I'd need some freedom. Like this." He looks around at the rest area parking lot like it is nirvana. "Nobody bothers me here," he says.

But people do bother us. There is a device in the truck called an Omnitrax, which is hooked up to the company headquarters by satellite, and there is a satellite receiver in the roof of the truck. The company can triangulate our exact location at any time. Ostensibly, this is for emergencies, in case we ever break down in a snowbank somewhere, but it is primarily used to stop the drivers from lying about their exact location in an effort to procure time off. Thus, a driver who wants a rest can't say, "Hi, I'm three hundred miles outside Seattle, be there tomorrow," when he is actually parked in a Seattle parking lot, having driven over the speed limit the whole night before. They'll just flick a switch and see his blinking light come up on a screen right where Seattle is, and fire him as soon as his truck is empty.

You can also type and receive messages on the Omnitrax, meaning that headquarters can communicate with us anytime they want. We periodically get notifications that items we have just dropped off have been nicked or scratched, and deductions are made from Jim's paychecks accordingly. Jim is responsible for everything. He is an independent contractor, but "independent" these days just means that nobody is paying for your health insurance.

Jim is suddenly worried that, when we see the lady again to drop off her stuff in Denver, I will smirk or look at her knowingly, now that I've seen naked pictures of her. I tell him not to worry about it, but I know he will.

We hit Denver, unload all her things into a storage space before the woman even shows up, have the warehouseman sign for it, and Jim calls the company and we take a day off. It is that easy. "You've been running pretty hard," they tell him. Somebody out there is a human being, a rare find these days. We spend the day milling around a picturesque college town, looking at girls and trying to find a place classy enough for us to get shitfaced.

The next day, I wake up and wander around some more, and I come upon a man with one hand trying to put a starter motor in his car. He asks me to help, and I spend a good amount of time slithering around in oil under the car, trying to bolt the motor into place. After about an hour of this we get it done, and he starts it up. He's got a car that works now, and I have a new appreciation of how good life is when you have two hands. I head back to the truck in a good mood.

Jim is awake and hungover, and my positive, easy-going attitude is infectious. "Let's just stay here another day," he says. We had a good time in the bars last night, and the mountains look peaceful. "I'll rent a suite in the nicest hotel in town. On me."

It's an enticing offer. Who am I to argue? "Can you afford it?"

"I've got a credit card."

"I don't want you to waste your money."

"I want to do this. I think we should have a good time out here, at least when we can. I appreciate you coming out here."

"Thanks." I am flattered.

So he rents a room in the finest hotel in Boulder, Colorado, that has a parking lot big enough to accommodate a tractor trailer. We get a suite, which gives us each a room, with our own TV and microwave and toilet. I like Jim, but living together without any personal space for two weeks is a strain on any relationship. I get to use a remote control for an hour or two without having it snatched out of my hands. I watch *Law and Order* with sound. It is bliss.

And that's all we do with our day off—sleep, rest up, flip channels, go to the bathroom. There's a lousy restaurant fifty feet away that we limp over to when we get hungry. Then it's nightfall. We fall asleep. Then it's daylight. We get back on the road.

We're on our way to Seattle, and Jim lets me drive through Wyoming because it's a wasteland. Wyoming has no trees or people, great advantages for a novice tractor trailer driver. There's nothing to hit if you run off the road. Other cars and trucks are only visible every twenty minutes or so. As he calls out instructions to me, I realize that Jim has a gift for teaching.

"Did you ever want to be a teacher?" I ask him.

"Yeah. After I got out the army, I looked into it."

"What happened?"

"I had a roommate who was a teacher. He made about eight dollars an hour. I was waiting tables at the time and I always had to lend him money. This guy had been to school for four years so he could borrow money from a waiter."

"Where is he now?"

"He's still teaching. He loves it. But he had to move back in with his folks. I'd like to teach too, but I don't think my folks would let me move back with 'em. Downshift."

"What?"

"We're coming to a hill here. You need to downshift."

I manage to do it without grinding the gears. I'm getting the hang of this thing. An hour or two later we pull into Sheridan, but I don't feel confident enough to back the truck into a space.

"We're going into Idaho tomorrow," he tells me. "I'll drive from now on."

The next day in Idaho, I see what happens when truckers drive themselves too hard. We are coming down a seven percent grade that goes on for miles, and I see rescue workers pulling a tractor trailer out of a ravine. Brake failures on these steep hills and windy, dark roads have killed more than a few drivers. A few miles on, there is another wreck, obviously fatal. I wonder, what was the last thing they thought as they went flying off the road? Were they thinking about the money they were making? About their logbooks? About wives or children? And then it all just turned to pure terror.

It is starting to get dark, and starting to snow. I look out the window for a while, staring at the clouds of moisture coming from the truck in front of us. If there's an ice patch, that guy'll hit it first, we'll get some warning. Jim doesn't seem concerned. He is just staring straight ahead, sunglasses on.

"It's almost dark," I suggest helpfully. "Maybe you could see better without the sunglasses."

He looks at me and nods. "I'll take 'em off in a little while."

I sit there quietly. The roar of the diesel engine and the hissing of the tires on the wet pavement is making me sleepy.

"If I fall asleep, you're gonna stay awake, right?"

Jim laughs. We'll either crash or we won't. Either way, I won't be a factor. I crawl into the sleeper and doze off.

We drop off in Seattle, our final load, and the truck is empty. We await further orders from the Omnitrax.

Nothing happens. Jim calls the head office, and we discover that nobody is moving out of Seattle for at least a few days. This means we have some time off, which is always nice, but for at least a few days there is no money to be made.

To Jim, I am no longer a helper. I am a hungry mouth to feed. When I am working seventy hours a week, it's not a problem to pay me $500 a week, but when I'm sitting on a bed in a motel on Interstate 5, I'm a bad investment. At this rate, I could suck his bank account dry in a matter of days.

I tell him not to pay me, just to lend me money until we get busy again, but he insists. Then he examines his bank statements again, and breaks out in a sweat. Then he tells me not to worry about it, that everything is going to be fine. Then he calls the office again and they tell him there's no one moving out of Seattle, but as soon as they get a job, they'll let him know. We get a bill from the motel for four days, almost $200. Poof, there's all the profit from one of the moves up in smoke. The unspoken reality of the situation is obvious. If I wasn't here, Jim wouldn't need to be staying in a motel, he could live in his sleeper and shower for five dollars a day in a truck stop.

"I'm going into town," I tell Jim on the fifth day. I wander into downtown Seattle, a city so progressive in its treatment of the homeless that homeless people have flocked here from all across the West. They pester me at the bus stop, at the deli where I stop in for a sandwich, and as I walk down the street. They are everywhere. If Jim drove off before I got back, I'd be one of them.

I head down to Rayford Seafoods, which hired me to work in Alaska back in college. It's a ramshackle office that belies the huge profits the fishing companies make.

"Are you looking for processors?" I ask the girl behind the counter.

She wordlessly hands me an application. I fill it out, the usual shit. My hobbies, where I went to grade school. I put "the moon" for grade school and "compulsive masturbation" as my hobby and no one notices.

She puts the application in a pile without reading it. "The plane leaves tomorrow morning for Dutch Harbor. Can you take a drug test at 3 P.M.?" I gather I've been hired.

They'll hire me on nothing but a drug test. That's Alaska work for you. They just don't care. They fly you up to Alaska at their expense, but if you don't finish out the contract you sign, they won't fly you back. They'll let you die in a snowdrift before you're allowed near the plane. It doesn't matter to them if you're wanted in five states, if you've quit your last thirty jobs, if you're homeless, an alcoholic, whatever. Get on the plane to Dutch Harbor and show 'em what you got, and if you don't, you're a dead man. Apparently, it does matter to them if you've smoked pot recently, or at least they pretend it does, because I am given an address where I can pee into a cup.

Drug testing is hilarious stuff, the last stand in America's mad love-hate relationship with drugs. I'd definitely prefer a pilot or a surgeon who wasn't high on something, but testing them every six months won't catch them anyway, or it might reveal that they've smoked something six weeks ago while on vacation. I'm sure the high has worn off by the time they sit in the cockpit or pull on the surgery gloves, which means that the testing itself is basically irrelevant.

What drug testing accomplishes is to strike fear into the hearts of bank tellers, meat packers, assembly line workers, desk clerks, football players, and fish processors. It's a great eliminator. The words "WE DRUG TEST" tend to keep out the riffraff, people who know they'd fail. My advice to those people is, try it anyway; they probably just dump your pee down the toilet and tell you whether you passed or failed, based on whether they liked you or not. I've smoked a joint on my way to a drug test and passed, and I've been clean for months and failed.

I take a bus over to the "clinic," a shack with a surgical table and a toilet. These people are sparing no expense in the war on drugs. They're hiring people who walk through the door without reading their applications. How demanding can this screening process be? Alaska work is like law school. They'll let anyone in, then weed you out later.

As we are milling around in the lobby, waiting for the bus to take us back to the city center, one girl anxiously asks the receptionist when we'll find out the results. That's always an act of genius. Why doesn't she just say, "Look, when do I find out if those Golden Seal tablets really work?" The receptionist tells her they won't let us on the plane at the airport if we've failed. Our pee has already been flushed, I'm sure of it.

Myself, I've spent so much time with Jim lately, who is drug-free because his company tests randomly, that I'm clean either way. More importantly, I've been polite to everyone. I know I'll pass.

I head back out to Highway 5 to tell Jim I just signed on with a fish-processing company and am flying to Alaska tomorrow morning.

"You didn't have to do that," he says, his eyes aglow with relief at seeing the last of me. He can check out of the motel now, throw all his stuff back into his sleeper and live in a parking lot. His future just got a lot brighter. Every day without work doesn't need to send him into a panic anymore.

"I appreciate your helping me out," he says.

"Likewise."

We shake hands, wish each other luck. I head down to the Seattle Youth Hostel with about twenty dollars left in my pocket. The homeless shadow me as I go out and spend half of it on beer.

Five hours later I am at the airport.

On the Slime Line

Rayford Seafoods in Dutch Harbor runs its whole operation out of a disused World War II LST that sits in chilly Iliulink Bay. The LST, which used to carry men into battle, has been converted into a crab-processing boat. Crab fishermen bring their freshly caught crab up to the boat and they are pumped on board, still alive. Here, the processors, of whom I am one, grab them and pull their legs off or blast their guts out with a water hose. Then they are boxed and frozen and sold to the Japanese.

Every crab caught in these waters is going straight to Japan because Americans won't pay high prices for fresh crab. Japanese buyers wander around while we are working, grabbing our arms to prevent us from pulling too hard on the crab legs, showing us how not to bruise the meat. Their manner is always abusive and rude. Sometimes, after a brief instruction session from a Japanese buyer, workers spit or blow their noses on the crabmeat before shoveling it off into the freezer.

The place where we work is a giant warehouse, the former hold of the ship. Windows and doors are open everywhere, allowing the cool, damp November air in. We bundle up. There is also seawater flying everywhere, and the cooking steam from the tons of packed crab legs that we drop into boiling vats produces a foul and abrasive odor that clings to our clothes and hair. Because of the wetness and smell, we wear plastic outer garments called rain gear.

The shifts are sixteen hours long, so a tiny pin prick sized hole in your rain gear can let enough water in over the course of a day to completely soak you by half-time. If you're working wet, you're one miserable bastard. Your clothes chafe against your skin, you're cold, and the wetness keeps expanding. By the time you take off your gear at the end of the shift, that same pin prick can let in enough water to completely fill your boots. So we try to keep the pin pricks down to a minimum.

I'm getting off work after my first shift, having just been flown in from Seattle that morning. There was no orientation, no ceremony. The crab are coming in and Rayford Seafoods isn't playing around.

Next to me, as I take off my rain gear, is an angry Filipino, flipping through the sheets of wet yellow-and-orange plastic to find someone else's rain gear. Our names are written on the gear in black marker. He finds what he is looking for, looks around quickly, and sticks it several times with a pin. Then he drops the pin on the floor and walks off, not looking at me.

Someone has pissed him off. Someone else's battle, not mine. I want to mind my own business and get to bed. I hang my gear on a hook and climb the stairs up to the bunk rooms.

The bunk rooms are similar to what I remember from old

movies of German prison camps, except in *Stalag 17* there wasn't always an inch of water on the floor. Also, in *Stalag 17* they had windows, and we're below decks. It's impossible to change your clothes without splashing your pant legs and soaking your feet, and when the lights are out, which is when anyone is sleeping, the room is blacker than a coal mine. And because we're on shift work, there's always someone sleeping.

The first morning, I forget about the water and put on my last pair of dry socks while still in my bunk, then soak them through the second I touch down. Then I try blundering over to the sliver of light that sneaks through the door to the passageway, or head, or galley, or whatever the hell they call a hallway on a ship, and bang my knee on something. So, my second day, I stand on the slime line with a swollen knee and wet feet for sixteen hours.

My roommates are a nineteen-year-old Klansman from Seattle, a muscular black man, and a white guy named Jeff who likes to start trouble. All of them own guns. I get finished after my second day and stumble up to my bunk to find Hale, the black guy, cleaning a pistol. Billy the Klansman is sleeping and Jeff is sitting on his bunk sharpening a hunting knife. Billy has drawn shut the curtain across his bunk. Jeff mimics throwing the knife into Billy's bunk, and Hale points the pistol and silently mouths, "Bang!" They look at each other and smile.

"How was work?" Hale asks me, as I crawl into my bunk and take off my pants.

"It's over."

"You like butchering crab?"

"Not much."

"You're a big guy. We got other jobs here."

"Like what?"

"Loading boxes in case-up." Case-up is a dream job compared to most of what Alaska offers. The work is physical, but I much prefer that to the standing still and monotony of conveyor belt line work. Best of all, it is dry. The crab are already cased by the time the boxes come down to case-up. The case-up crew packs them into freezers or, even better, loads them onto a Japanese freighter, which means you get to work outside. I've only been here two days and figured case-up jobs went to people who'd worked here for months, even years.

"You want a case-up job?" Hale asks.

"Hell, yeah."

"I'm the supervisor of the deck crew," he says. "I'll talk to Rick tomorrow."

The next day, I'm standing on the slime line when the Filipino woman next to me smiles at me. "What is your name?" she asks.

I tell her, and we chat for a while as we pack the crab crates. She has been in America for six months and is trying to learn English, and she asks me to teach her some words for various things. Chatting, even in tortured English, makes the time go by quicker. We break for lunch, and I go up to the lunchroom and sit at the Americans' table, which is fairly small, and she walks by and smiles at me.

"You'd better watch out," one guy tells me. "Don't be talking to her." This guy, who I know as Mike, is a big, bearded bear of a man, a truck driver from Seattle who has lost his driver's license after a drunk driving conviction. He's up here for a year, until he gets it back.

"Why not?"

"Her husband's crazy. He works down on the slime line too. He'll punch holes in your rain gear if he sees you talking to her."

"Just talking?"

"Just talking. I was teaching her some English last week, and I came back from break and my gear was all punched full of holes. Just a theory, but I think that's what happened."

A Filipino walks by, looks at me, the same fellow I had seen punching holes in the rain gear the first night on the boat, and I nod to Mike.

"That him?"

"That's him."

"He did punch holes in your gear. I saw him do it."

Now this guy is pissed. "Why the fuck didn't you say something?"

"To who? I had just gotten off the plane. I didn't know what I was getting involved in."

He shrugs. "Guarantee you, when you go back to work after lunch, you got holes in your gear."

"Let's get the fucker."

"Right on."

Sure enough, I get back from lunch and my gear has about ten pin pricks in it. We are all gearing up to walk back to the slime line, and the little Filipino fellow walks past me without saying a word. While people are pulling on their rain gear all around me, I rear back and thump him on the head. He falls forward, then springs up, enraged. He is about to charge me when Mike grabs him from behind. The whole thing is spontaneous, but it looks beautifully choreographed. Mike is holding him and I rip into him, pummeling away at his ribs and face for about five seconds, then I stop, Mike lets go, he falls to the floor, and we both step over him.

As I am walking away, I notice a group of Filipinos who were too surprised by the speed of the whole incident to step forward and stop it. I am aware of their eyes as I walk back to the slime line.

I am packing crates again, this time with two Americans standing next to me, when I get a tap on the shoulder. It is Rick, the line supervisor.

"Take your rain gear off, get a coat, and go topside. Help with the loading."

I leave immediately. I peel off my gloves, my now worthless rain gear full of tiny pin pricks, my boots, all the plastic and rubber crap issued to me the moment I got off the plane, deducted from my first paycheck. The gloves I toss in a big metal glove bin. The rain gear goes in the trash. I am aware that the Filipinos are still watching me as I walk out.

Topside there is fresh air and none of the factory noise—the air compressors, the forklifts, the constant whirring of the hydraulic lifts. It is actually a nice day, I am surprised to see. Working down in the hold and sleeping down below decks, it is possible to go for days without seeing sunlight. We are allowed to leave the ship when we are not on shift, but no one really has the energy. Straight to the mess and then straight to bed.

Hale and Jeff greet me on the foredeck. "What's going on, man?"

"Not much. What's going on up here?"

"Taking a break," Hale laughs. He and Jeff have just been sitting on the rigging, listening to the sounds of the bay, with the factory noise filtering up from below. "Hang out with us a little while."

I sit on a pile of boxes and look out at the bay, hundreds of seagulls flying around, pecking the water for the waste products of crab processing.

"Watch the seagulls," Hale says, pointing. So I stare at a

crowd of seagulls milling around on the surface, picking bits of
waste out of the water with quick head thrusts. I'm not sure
what I'm looking for. Suddenly, a sea lion silently shoots up
from below, grabs one, and submerges again before I am really
sure what I have just seen.

"Whoa," I say.

"Isn't that cool?" Hale and Jeff are alive with excitement.
"That fucker must have eaten about ten of them so far. And
they just sit there and take it."

The rest are down below, sweating, chafing, ready to kill each
other, splashed with water, inhaling crab steam, while these two
jokers hang out on the deck and watch wildlife. "Is this what
you guys do all day?"

"Naw, man. We're gettin' busy in a bit. We gotta load that
freighter." Hale points to an ancient Korean rust bucket pulling
up alongside. "Wanna help?"

"Sure."

"We'll be ready to go in about an hour. In the meantime, just
hang out."

I sit on the deck for a few minutes, and guilt starts to set in.
Those guys are down there, begging for a break, their feet soaking, their knees pain wracked from standing still for hours on
end. Who am I to have been rescued from it? Who are these
two, to never have been through it at all? The Filipino woman I
spoke to before break will work her whole contract without getting an easy shift. Her English is no good and she isn't big
enough to work an off-load.

But for now, it feels too good to be dry, and topside. I lean
back in the rigging, which is as comfortable as a hammock, and
begin to doze. On the clock.

After an hour or two, I am woken up and we start loading.
The stacked pallets of fresh, boxed, and frozen crab are taken
up to the foredeck on a hydraulic lift. There I attach a rope

around the pallet and hook it to the crane from the Korean ship. Then it is hoisted over to their deck, where it is unhooked, and the crane comes back. Ten or twenty Korean laborers break the pallet apart and load the boxes into their hold.

All my job entails is hooking the rope and giving the Korean crane operator the thumbs-up. I also have to make sure we don't go too fast, dropping too many pallets on the Korean ship before they can unload them. Primarily, I'm in charge of the rhythm for the whole off-load. It's an easy enough job. It is a wet and windy day, but the beautiful scenery, the barren and forbidding mountains overlooking Dutch Harbor, make it a pleasure to be outside.

Nightfall comes around four o'clock in the afternoon, and we work until well past midnight. When the hold of the Korean ship is full, the sailors come over onto our ship and offer us a tour of their boat. Apparently, this is some kind of courtesy. All the off-loads involve a quick boat tour, I am told. I walk around for a while on a ship that makes ours look like the *Queen Mary*. Their living quarters are more cramped and claustrophobic than I could have ever imagined, rust is on everything. I look into their sick bay, where I see the cutting edge of Korean surgical equipment, a rusty knife hanging from a string. Then they offer us warm sodas, which we accept, because unopened Korean Coke bottles have collector's value.

"We don't have it so bad," I say to Jeff and Hale as we clamber back aboard the *Rayford*. "Those poor guys live like animals."

"You should see the Russian ships," Jeff tells me. "That's nothing. One of the Russian sailors was saying that sometimes their companies don't even feed them. They have to break open the crab boxes to eat if they run out of food."

We go down into the galley and have a late meal. Burgers, french fries, rice, all kinds of Asian delicacies as the cooks are Filipinos. I load up on carbohydrates and settle back, bloated, like an old man after a Thanksgiving meal. In the galley, we have cable TV from a satellite station, and I watch half an hour of CNN before heading to bed. It's good to be an American, even on the bottom rung.

I soon find out that there's a price to pay for not laboring in the factory.

I'm not working the deck crew, I'm being welcomed into a brotherhood. There are things going on here that I'd rather not know about, and I'm no longer able to just mind my own business.

"If something happens to me or Hale," Jeff asks me one day, his voice full of drama. "Would you back us up?"

I'm not sure what I'm being asked. I imagine he's asking me about natural disasters, falling into the icy water or being attacked by a sea lion. "Of course," I tell him.

He looks at me as if he can't really believe me, the overlong stare of someone who wants you to understand the gravity of a conversation, like a lover seeking commitment. He's creeping me out. "Do you know what I mean?" he asks again.

"Uh, sure."

He is not satisfied. He wanders off with a new and clearly lower opinion of me. I already sense that there is some kind of criminal venture going on aboard this ship, something that involves the off-load crew, and if they want to tell me about it, fine. If not, that's also good. I'll decide whether I want to get involved based partly on what little conscience I have left, and partly on the plan's feasibility. But as I live and work with them, it's going to be hard for them not to include me.

Later in the day, while I am tying ropes on the foredeck, I meet a rough, overweight older man with the drawn skin of a heavy drinker and the rumpled appearance of someone who has slept under a bridge. He wears a black windbreaker, torn in places, which has the name of an Anchorage tittie bar emblazoned on the back in faded red letters.

"Jeff or Hale around?" he asks. He has a voice like a chainsaw.

"Haven't seen 'em in a bit."

"Where the fuck they go?"

"Couldn't tell you."

He waddles off.

A few minutes later, Jeff and Hale come back.

"There was a guy here looking for you a little while ago."

"What did he look like?"

I describe him.

"Did he seem pissed off?"

"A little bit."

This freaks them out. They ask me ten questions about the guy, mostly concerning his attitude and mental state. Did he seem this way, did he seem that way? The encounter was too brief and insignificant for me to remember the type of detail they need, and they become annoyed with me.

"You need to pay attention," Jeff tells me.

"Maybe the next time you guys wander off you can tell me where the fuck you're going," I snap. They look at each other, curious, then back down. I'm usually quiet and polite, at least by Alaskan standards.

Hale explains, "That guy makes about five million dollars a year."

"He looks like a street person."

This amuses them, a little bit. They laugh harder than necessary to let me know that all is well between us again. I laugh too. Oh, what fun we are having.

These guys are nuts.

I'm surrounded by crazy people, and I deal with it by pretending not to notice. Thus, when Billy the Klansman, our fourth roommate, starts ranting at me one afternoon when I come back on break about how we should send all black people back to Africa, I nod and smile. He then cranks up a Guns n' Roses tape, and when Axl Rose screams the word "niggers," he turns the volume up louder, then back down again when the n-word is complete. He looks at me conspiratorially. I nod back and smile. My main complaint with Billy the Klansman is not his politics (we work so much that I hardly ever have to see him) but his bathing habits. This boy showers less than once a week, and the smells emanating from his bunk are starting to fill the whole room.

Billy is a skinny nineteen-year-old acne-ridden kid from Seattle who hates everybody else on the ship. He hates Mexicans and Filipinos and blacks and American Indians, the four groups that make up ninety-five percent of Rayford Seafoods' workforce. He hates Jeff because Jeff is always hanging around with Hale, who is black, and he calls him "nigger-lover" behind his back. He hates his father, who brought him up here, because he brought him up here. He hates women because they won't sleep with him, or even talk to him. All he talks about is how much he hates everyone, and he doesn't shower.

Billy's father is the boat's electrician, and Billy is supposed to be learning the trade. Half the electrical wires on the boat are under an inch of water and short circuits are so common that we hardly notice anymore when whole rooms suddenly become as black as a coal mine. Most of us have learned to carry around Zippos. The minute we hear a sizzling sound coming from behind the walls, we reach for our lighters and try to continue what we were doing. Like most people, Billy has a love-hate relationship with his job, from which the love has mostly gone.

"This job FUCKING SUCKS!" he screams one day as he enters the room. He rants about the hopelessness of trying to find and replace all the rusted-out fuse boxes, waterlogged wires, and damp connections all over this half-sunk vessel. Oil seeps through half the cracking rivets; seawater seeps through the other half. Sometimes tiny fish even get through the cracks, and they swim around in the bowels of the ship where Billy spends a lot of his time. He is close to crying as he describes this to me. I don't care. Alaska work is like that. Not pleasant. At least he gets to move around the ship, not get stuck on the slime line doing the same thing for sixteen hours at a stretch. When Jeff and Hale enter the room, he goes quiet, thankfully, and draws the curtain on his bunk and lies there.

Billy doesn't hate me because I treat him like what he is, a scared, weak little kid. I listen to him whine as long as it doesn't cost me anything. I tell him to take a shower and take his sheets to the laundry, and on occasion he does it. Unlike everyone else, I don't wish him harm. I just wish he would disappear.

When Billy's whining, I figure he isn't dangerous since at least he's trying to communicate. He's too scared of Jeff and Hale to insult them to their faces, and Jeff and Hale don't want trouble with him because his father is the chief electrician and could have them fired off the boat and sleeping in the snow within minutes. So there is a delicate balance, and sometimes there are innocuous conversations about music or home. Billy likes G n' R, Hale likes rappers, Jeff likes heavy metal, and I listen through my curtains as they debate the points of each. Sometimes it seems as if we could all just get along, like Jesus and Rodney King suggest.

All of a sudden the police kick the door in and officers in bulletproof vests are pulling my curtains back and pointing pistols at me.

"Let me see your hands," one of them screams. I show him my hands.

"Is Hale Jeffries here?"

"Who?"

"What bunk is he in?"

"Who?"

"Here he is," says another cop. "Here he is."

Their voices are excited and scared. "Get up!" One cop is screaming. "Lie down!" screams another. "Let me see your hands!" they shout in unison. There is a loud thump as they drag Hale from his second-tier bunk and dump him on the floor like a sack of potatoes. Then they stand him up and handcuff him, and walk toward the door.

"You!" one of the cops says, pointing at me. "You pull a stunt like that again, you're going to jail!" All I know is that thirty seconds ago I was half asleep in my bunk. Then they file out.

The room is quiet. Nobody wants to be the first to speak. Jeff gets up and closes the door, so it is dark again.

We're still working. We still need sleep. Crab is still coming in. After a few minutes of silence, I drift back off to sleep.

And here's how the inevitable trouble starts.

Hale, a muscular, tough-talking black street kid from Seattle, has spent the last few weeks talking shit about all the people he wasted and robbed while he was with a Seattle street gang. It sounded like bullshit to me, but I certainly wasn't going to call him on it. I didn't really care. Alaskan relationships are as substantial as meetings on a bus. You meet, bullshit them, then, when your contract is up, you go back to the world where you take up your life, most likely a different life from the one you have been describing to your Alaskan coworkers for the past five months. For example, I work with an illiterate drunk named Mo who tells me he went to Harvard, though another worker recognizes him as a frequent cohabitant of the local drunk-tank in Coeur d'Alene, Idaho. It doesn't matter. No one's doing background checks. As long as he doesn't start insulting anyone's intelligence with the Harvard stories, we all just let it go and expect the same courtesy with our own bullshit.

But it seems that Hale got a little carried away with a story, and someone in the Rayford office took notice and actually did a background check, where they found he was wanted by the Seattle police. Not for murder, as it turns out, but homosexual prostitution. The rumor files down the food chain quickly, and soon Jeff, who has spent every waking minute palling around with this self-proclaimed tough guy, is the target of ridicule.

Jeff has to deal not only with the misery of losing his best friend, but also with becoming the butt of every joke on the ship. Jeff owns a gun, for some reason. Billy also owns a gun. Billy, who I was starting to tolerate, becomes braver with his racist views now that he no longer lives with a muscular black man. Every time I enter the room after a shift, I am expecting a cross fire.

The fun finally gets out of hand during the Christmas party, where all these volatile elements are introduced to alcohol. Billy starts the evening off by getting rejected by a Mexican girl, which sends him into a tailspin of rage and depression. He goes off looking for Jeff, and finds him talking to a girl at the bottom of the gangway leading onto the *Rayford*.

"Nigger fag lover!" he screams. I'm not really sure what happens next, even though I'm watching. There is a lot of activity and Billy starts screaming. Two Mexican men come running over. Jeff is pounding Billy's head into a railing, and instead of putting a stop to it, which I am anticipating, the two start kicking him in the ribs. This is not a man who has made a lot of friends during his stay here at Rayford. I finally go down the ramp and say weakly, "Hey you guys, you're gonna kill him."

They look up at me.

"I think he's learned his lesson," I say. Billy is nearly unconscious at this point, and the snow all around is spattered with
blood.

Jeff snorts and walks off. The Mexicans are laughing and
continue stomping on Billy for a few more seconds, then they
walk past me as if I'm not there and clamber up the gangway.
Billy, bleeding in the snow, starts wailing and sobbing like a
foghorn. I'm deciding whether I should carry his blood-soaked
smelly body up the ramp when one of the ship's welders, a guy
named Tony, comes up behind me.

"Hey man, I'm going into Dutch for a drink. Wanna join me?"

"Sure."

"Who's that?" He points to Billy, screaming and bleeding in
the snow.

"My roommate."

"The electrician's kid?"

"Yeah."

We stand over Billy, regarding him with detached objectivity
as he thrashes around, wailing.

"Cab's waiting," says Tony.

The fun has only just begun.

Tony is a welder, one of the guys with his own cabin, and he
makes over $80,000 a year. Some mundane skill that could
barely pay for a one-bedroom apartment in the Bronx can earn
you more money than God in Alaska. The catch is that the
welders have to sign a one-year contract because these fishing
vessels that are rusting away need an on-site welder at all
times, and the companies don't want to be in the position of
hiring a new one every few months. The other thing about
contractual work is that fifty percent of the wage comes upon
completion of the contract. The companies know that if they

make the contract challenging, they get about half their welders for half-price, because a lot of them decide they've had enough of Dutch Harbor before their twelve months are up, and beg to go home. So the welders are some of the highest-paid men on the island, and most of them, I discover, are going slowly mad.

A year is too long to be up here. I can see how it begins, though. Some guy is happily welding away in Seattle, making his fourteen dollars an hour and living in a nice one-bedroom apartment, when some joker comes up and says, "Hey, I hear that up in Alaska they're paying welders $80,000 a year." After the disbelief, the guy shrugs and says, sign me up. So the happy welder flies off to Dutch Harbor, dreaming of riches, and three months later he's showing signs of madness after having been locked away on a rusting vessel that requires more welding than he could ever have imagined.

I don't know this when I agree to go out for a beer with Tony. I think of Tony as a nice family man who welds for a living, and he might be a nice change from Jeff and Billy. We are in the cab heading for the Unisea Bar when he pulls out a pistol and says, "Hold this for me."

"Okay." I hold his pistol for him. I figure he just needs to adjust his pants or something, then he'll ask for it back, but he's staring out the window as if he's just asked me to hold his wallet. "Why am I holding your pistol?" I ask after a minute.

"We just have to stop off and get some shit from this Filipino guy. I'd rather you had the gun in case they try anything on me."

"Okay." I'm not sure what "shit" means or what "try anything" could indicate, but I think it might be best if I had the pistol because I'm the most rational person around. I don't have a holster, and I certainly don't want to de-ball myself by shoving it into my hip pocket, so after we get out of the cab I find myself walking around with it in my hand.

This doesn't seem to bother Tony. He likes having a gun-wielding sidekick. We climb the ramp of another processing ship and he turns to me and says, "Wait here. If you hear anything, come in with that thing firing."

"Sure thing."

He enters a room, and through the door, before it closes behind him, I see a group of Filipino men lounging around on bunks. It is a ship's watertight door, so even if they are strangling Tony, which they appear too lazy to do, I wouldn't be able to hear a thing. I hang around by the ship's rail, taking in the night scenery, watching a gentle snowfall over the bay.

This is probably a drug deal, and most likely will be a quietly successful one, but Alaska allows people's imaginations to run away with them. Instead of being a tired welder who wants to score some coke for a Christmas bash, Tony has decided he's an underworld operator. He's got his sidekick outside the door, "packing," waiting for the deal to "go bad." I've become an actor in his little play for the evening. What I wanted was a few beers, a good conversation, maybe to run into one of those rare creatures in Dutch Harbor, a woman. Now I'm caught up in another manufactured drama. The long hours, the lack of women (only one person in ten is female), and the transient nature of the work all lend themselves to an idea that we are living out some macho fantasy. Teenagers come here to make money for college and wind up swigging Wild Turkey straight from a bottle, standing shirtless on a mountaintop, recounting imaginary exploits with sex-starved cheerleaders. I'm just about to walk down the ramp and go home when Tony opens the door, gives me a knowing nod, and we're off to the pubs.

A good percentage of the cab drivers in Dutch Harbor are pretty Filipino women, and they often have a side business giving blow jobs. The cab driver who picks us up this time is beautiful, and Tony starts inquiring about the possibilities.

"Some of the girls do that," she tells him, "but I don't. I have boyfriend."

"One hundred dollars," Tony tells her. "That's twice the going rate."

She laughs, but doesn't agree.

"One twenty-five."

"Thank you, but no."

"How many rides would you have to give to make one hundred fifty dollars?"

She waves at him, trying to get him to stop talking, but he persists. We pull up outside the Unisea Bar and I make to get out, but Tony turns to me and says, "I'll meet you inside." I shrug, hop out, and go inside, order myself a beer. Through the glass door, I can see him still debating with the cab driver. Finally, he gets out and the cab drives off.

"Fucking bitch," he tells me. "Let's shoot some pool."

We get involved in a pool game with two Mexican fishermen, for twenty dollars a game. We win the first one, then the second, and Tony starts taunting them. He calls them both "Pedro" and talks to them like Speedy Gonzales, in a nasal whine with a bad Mexican accent. "You meesed your shot, man," he says every time one of them muffs a chance. Then it is Tony's turn, and he scratches on the eight ball.

I pull ten dollars out of my pocket and hand it to one of the Mexicans. "Don't pay him, man," Tony tells me. "They bumped the table."

"Come on, Tony. We lost."

Tony starts walking away, not ready to cough up his ten bucks. One of the Mexicans cracks him in the mouth with a pool cue, and a tooth comes flying out and lands on the green felt of the pool table. I'm looking at the tooth while they continue to pummel him. Nobody else in the bar gives the scene much attention. This is an hourly occurrence.

"The piece, man, pull out the piece!" Tony thinks I should start shooting these men because they got mad when he tried to cheat them at pool.

I utter my superhero tag line, "I'm outta here," and walk toward the door while the Mexicans continue to whack him with cues. I step outside and enjoy a cigarette, and thus end my association with Tony the Welder. The nice family man who welded for a living.

That's how it is up here. Everyone is fucked up, and those who aren't soon will be. The mayor should figure out how to say that in Latin and make it the town motto. Or better yet, "Dutch Harbor: What fatal flaw in your character made you wind up here?"

What does that say about me, I wonder? For me, like most of us, it is the panic-ridden quest to stay afloat that brings me up here. The fact that I live on a boat that actually appears to be sinking is merely coincidental irony. Dutch Harbor offers the opportunity to make money while keeping your expenses at a minimum. Say what I like about my waterlogged room, it is free, as is my food and electricity. Every dollar we make up here goes to us, not to landlords or utilities or bill collectors. That is the real freedom, and it's a freedom that a lot of us can't handle.

Two drunk fishermen come up to me as I am peacefully puffing my cigarette, watching the snowfall.

"Hey man, you work on the decks at Rayford, right?"

"Yeah."

"Our bunkhouse is down near Rayford, and we're too drunk to drive. Can you help us out? It'll save you cab fare."

"You just need a ride back?"

"Yeah."

One of them hands me the keys and we climb inside a battered, rusted, red pick-up. I haven't been in a car in months, and I like the feel of it. I drive off carefully through the snow while the fishermen laugh raucously with one another, recounting events from what was obviously a wild evening.

Within seconds, blue lights are flashing behind me. I'm getting pulled over by a cop in Dutch Harbor on Christmas Eve.

"Don't worry about it," one of the fishermen tells me. "I've got three DUIs, and this cop knows my truck."

"Great. Thanks for mentioning that earlier."

The cop shines the flashlight in on us, looks around the cab. "Step out of the vehicle, sir," he says to me.

I step out.

"Can I see your license?"

I hand him my truck driver's learner's permit from North Carolina, the only thing I have handy. They're good for three months, and mine has expired. "What's this?"

I start to tell him, but he ignores me and has me start the nose-touching and alphabet-reciting of a drunk test. I hop around on one foot for a few seconds.

"How do you know Tom?" he asks.

"He just came up to me, asked for a ride home. His bunkhouse is near my ship."

He asks me more personal questions about where I work, my social security number, and so on. Finally he lets me go.

"That guy's a cocksucker," Tom tells me when I get back in the truck. "He's always hassling me."

I drive back to Rayford, park the truck, and go to bed.

The next day, I'm lying in bed when the chief electrician, Billy's father, comes in and asks to talk to me.

"What's up?" He looks serious.

"I wanted to thank you," he tells me. "For saving my son's

life." He extends a sincere hand to me and I shake it. "Billy told me the story of what happened."

The last I saw Billy, I left him screaming and bleeding in the snow while I went off to get a beer. By not actually helping to kill him, I have become the Florence Nightingale of the ship.

Then two police officers come in behind him, the two who arrested Hale a few days ago. "Mr. Levison?"

"Yeah?"

"This is a notice to appear in court four days from now. You've been charged with driving without a license."

"You're charging me with driving without a license?"

"Yes. We expect you in court or a warrant will be issued."

"You're kidding."

They leave, after tossing an official looking piece of paper on my bed. I can now define irony. During an evening in which I witnessed two felony beatings, a drug deal, firearms possession, and public drunkenness, I am told to appear in court for giving someone a ride home.

Dutch Harbor is like the third grade when the New Age substitute teacher showed up. Nobody is really in charge. But the Dutch Harbor police, I soon discover, have a habit of grabbing one turd a week in the sea of shit that is their town, and trying to make an example of him. Thus, gay prostitute Hale is flown all the way back to Seattle to stand trial, and ride-giver Iain is jerked away from the deck crew for an entire day to face the music. Their philosophy is, you gotta start somewhere.

On the good side, there are my coworkers' reactions. Far from endangering my position with Rayford, having cops come on board and toss a writ at me makes me something of an outlaw legend. I discover that most of the deck crew already knows about my fistfight with the Filipino who sieved my rain gear, and being pursued by armed men for a minor driving offense has only added to my mystique. Thus, I am asked about it by almost everyone. "What did the cops want?" It's hard not to embellish. By the time I'm through mildly adjusting the facts, I'm a Robin Hood type wanted in thirty states for trying to save the rain forest.

On the down side, we have just started shift work again after Christmas, and I am working twelve-hour shifts at night. This means, in order to make my court appearance, I am going to have to miss an entire day's sleep. The courthouse is about five miles away, and I spent all my cash over Christmas, so I'm going to have to walk each way after working twelve hours the night before. Even to get the court date postponed, so that I could attend on a day when there is no crab coming in, I still have to show up in court. They won't give me a continuance over the phone. So if I'm going to go all the way down there, I might as well go to trial.

My day comes, and I walk through the slush and mud of Dutch Harbor. Under different circumstances, this could be a beautiful and interesting town. There are bunkers left over from World War II spotting the shoreline, majestic mountains overlooking the town. Strings of mist circle around the crab boats tied up to the docks.

I discover, during my walk, that Dutch Harbor actually has a college campus, the University of Alaska at Dutch Harbor. UADH is a shack, much like my grandfather's tool shed. The town library is a Quonset hut. The courthouse is a mud-spattered wooden structure on the far side of the town.

But inside, there is no difference from any other small town courthouse. There are wanted posters on the wall, and the ever-present bored secretary sitting behind a plywood desk, looking at a computer screen. She asks me my name and motions for me to be seated on a small bench.

I watch the trial before mine, a fisherman who has been caught with half an eighth of marijuana in his bunkhouse.

Apparently, he came home and found his wife in bed with another fisherman and a fight ensued, and the wife called the police. Law enforcement's contribution to the whole affair was to rummage around and find the pot, for which they then arrested him. Talk about a bad day. The judge shares my sympathy, but Alaska has only recently outlawed marijuana. Up until a few months ago, it was legal here to possess an eighth of an ounce or less, and now they are trying to make examples of people who have not adhered to the new laws. Five hundred dollars and five hundred hours of community service.

Next, the people of Alaska versus Iain Levison, unlicensed driver. The judge asks me if I knew my license had expired. I know how to answer that, but it doesn't help. What amazes me is that in this dirt-water town, this lawless backwash of civilization where people wear tourist T-shirts that say "Dutch Harbor . . . it's not the end of the world, but you can see it from here," someone has run my driver's license through a computer and determined that it has expired.

"I'm not going to fine you," she tells me, "but you have to do some community service. The penalty here for driving without a license is unusually harsh because people come up here and think they can get away with anything." Sure. Of course. Look around you, sister, they *are* getting away with anything.

"Five hundred hours." She bangs her gavel, like they do in *Law and Order*. She shuffles some papers and nods for the next case.

Five hundred hours. That's about twelve weeks of free work I have to contribute to Dutch Harbor, while I am working a minimum of eighty-four hours a week at Rayford. The only way to manage this would be to never sleep.

I ask the secretary what community service involves, and she tells me that it's mostly stuff with the harbormaster's office, driving around picking up dead sea lions that are rotting on the shoreline, that sort of thing. I ask her if there's anything available at the library. She shakes her head. The library already has two full-time employees. The only thing they need right now is outdoor work, which means physically demanding. And at the end of the day at Rayford, I'm out of gas.

I walk back to Rayford and I find Jeff packing up the last of his things. He has been fired for thumping Billy.

"What're you gonna do?"

"Go home. I've made two thousand. I can't afford the plane ticket, I'll have a little left over." The airfare back and forth from Seattle is astronomical. Most fishing companies will pay it round trip if you finish your contract, but if you get fired or quit, you're on your own.

I like Jeff and I realize I'll miss him. He's a little out of control sometimes, caught up in the macho fantasy world that this lifestyle creates, but he has a good sense of humor.

"Why don't you try to get a job with one of the boats?"

He shakes his head. "I've had enough of this shit."

I know what he means. No one here with enough money for plane fare home is really that distraught about getting fired. You get back to the world, back to towns with women, where the men say, "Excuse me," when they bump into you in bars, where everything doesn't smell like fish or steamed crab, and people wear something besides rain gear. And if you're fired, you don't have to think of yourself as a failure for quitting.

"I'm gonna have to leave myself pretty soon. I got five hundred hours of community service for driving those fishermen around. There's no way I can do that. And I barely have enough saved for a ticket. If I jetted out right now, I'd be flat broke in Seattle, which is why I came up here in the first place."

He snorts. "Five hundred hours. What a fucking joke."

We shake hands. The door closes. I have six hours to sleep before I have to work a twelve-hour shift.

My new roommates are Rus and Colin, two college kids who are a refreshing, clean-cut change from the social pathology that I have become accustomed to. They seem young and energetic and find things like the water on the floor a charming change from their middle-class environments. They think Dutch Harbor is an exciting place, and their first day here they buy a book about the Japanese invasion of the Aleutians during World War II.

"Come upstairs," Rus tells me breathlessly as I am lying in my bunk. "You gotta see this!"

"What?"

"Just come on."

I've only just laid down, but I figure this must be something great, so I pull my boots on and follow him. We go out on to the foredeck, where Colin is holding the book open and looking at the mountains.

"Look at this," Colin tells me excitedly. He points to a photograph in the book that shows Japanese bombers swarming over Dutch Harbor. "The mountain formations in this picture are exactly the same as the mountain formations right there. This happened right here, right where we're standing!"

I nod. "Cool," I say politely, and head back to my bunk.

This is how these kids are about everything. Even the crappy Filipino food we are given to eat is intriguing and new. Rus, who didn't bring enough money with him to buy tourist crap, asks to borrow $100 so he can go shopping in town and send stuff back to his folks. I lend it to him because he lives with me and he's not going anywhere and I know he has a job. Then, their second night at work, Colin falls off the dock into the water.

This is Alaska in midwinter. The water in the harbor is so cold that if they don't fish you out in a matter of seconds, your muscles freeze up and you just slip beneath the surface. Colin's in the water for about ninety seconds. They get him, and the next time I see him he's physically okay, but he doesn't think everything is amazing anymore.

"This place fucking sucks," he tells me two days later. Ru: has picked up on this too. It was bound to happen. The water incident just sped things along. Dutch Harbor is not a vacation spot, and treating it like one doesn't make it the Bahamas. The next day I get off shift, go down to my room, and their bunks are empty.

I go up to the office. "What happened to those two guys in my room?" I ask.

"Family emergency. Had to fly 'em back today." The office guy has more important things to think about.

"Were they related?"

"Said they were cousins."

"They weren't cousins. They were college roommates. They told me they only met each other last year."

"I'm just telling you what they told me," he says.

"Fucker owed me $100."

"I'll tell you what. Before I send anyone else home, I'll check with you first." This guy is more sarcastic than I am. He has heard every bullshit story in the book. But he adds, almost sympathetically, "We verified it with a phone call home."

It's never hard to find a sister or girlfriend to pretend to be a grieving relative of two guys who aren't even related. I wander back down to my bunk, where I now have one of the largest bunk rooms on the ship all to myself. Another $100 lesson learned. The lessons are piling up.

With Jeff and Hale gone, I'm now the chief of the deck crew. For that matter, I'm the entire deck crew. The deck boss goes and gets me two college kids fresh off the plane to help load pallets.

One of them, a slight, fresh-faced all-American named Chris, was working on his father's mink farm in Oregon a week ago when he suddenly decided he wanted a change. He got his wish. He looks a tad slight for the physical work, but he seems pleasant enough.

The other is a big, muscular frat boy named Brian who wants to "make money to buy nice things." Someone told him you can make a ton of money in Alaska. He knows everything about loading pallets, he knows everything about mackerel, he knows everything about Koreans, with whom we are working. He knows everything about everything and takes to the job eagerly. From the size of him, I figure he'll find this type of work easy enough.

After five hours of loading pallets, Brian is worn out and starts complaining. This type of work is hard on the muscles when you first start, and you need to pace yourself. Even if you're in good shape, it'll still wear you down. The boxes aren't light and they have to be placed a certain way, then they have to be shrink-wrapped to prevent them from sliding when they go up on the crane. Lifting and stacking the boxes is the easy part; the shrink-wrapping is a bitch because you have to bend down and run backwards in circles around the pallet, holding a heavy roll of clear plastic wrap that makes an explosive noise as it unravels. The pallets are over six feet high when fully stacked, so on the last few rotations around the pallet, you have to hold the plastic wrap over your head, which wears out your arms in a hurry.

All this has to be done in a rush, to keep the flow of the off-load going smoothly. If Brian and Chris fail to wrap the top boxes carefully, they'll go spilling into the water between the two ships. Each sixty-pound box of crab legs is worth hundreds of dollars, so it's my job to make sure this doesn't happen.

"We need to take a break," Brian tells me, panting, as another load of boxes comes out of the hold on the hydraulic lift. He's only been here a day, so he doesn't get it yet. You just don't say things like that. It's a given that everybody working on the ship needs to take a break at any given time, but the break times are scheduled, and not scheduled often.

"Just a few more pallets," I tell him. "Then it's break time."

"I need a break now."

The workers in the hold are waiting for me to get this new load of boxes off the lift so they can bring it back down and load more. I don't have time to argue with him, so I hand him the tally clipboard, which I am using to count the boxes coming out of the hold.

"Take this," I tell him. "We'll switch out for a bit."

I help Chris, who hasn't complained at all, and we finish off the next few pallets before we take a break. When our break is over, I decide it's not fair to give Brian a break and keep Chris working just because Brian whined, so I offer the tally sheet to Chris, to give him an easy hour or two.

Brian starts complaining again.

"Look," I tell him. "You've got the easiest job there is. You could be down on the slime line pulling crabs' legs off for twelve hours. Do you want that?"

"Yes, if I don't have to use this plastic wrap any more," he pants.

"Just a couple more hours, then see. We've just got to get this off-load finished."

It takes seven more hours, and Brian whines the whole time. When it's over, we go to the break room where they have a pay phone, and Brian heads right over to it.

"That's a satellite phone," I warn him. "It's not hooked up to a land line. It costs ten dollars a minute. If you want to make a call, you're better off going into town."

He shrugs and goes over to make the call.

The crew supervisor comes over and asks me how the guys he sent me are working out.

"Big guy's useless. Send him down to the slime line. The little guy's a keeper."

"Yeah, that's what I expected. The ones that won't shut up never do too well. Hell of a waste of all that muscle."

The next day, I get a tiny Mexican named Jorge who works like a maniac and never says a word. Brian is sent down to the slime line to pull crabs' legs off for twelve hours a day. Ironically, we don't have a ship coming in to pick up an off-load, so we spend most of the day milling around, cleaning up the deck, finding busy work.

"I don't think I can make enough money here," says Chris. He's only been in Alaska two days, but he's already researched the jobs enough to know that processing on board the *Rayford* puts him at the bottom of the Alaskan pay scale. We make five dollars an hour and get most of our money in overtime because by Alaskan law, anything over eight hours a day is overtime. Working eighty-four hours a week, which is light by Alaskan standards, gives us $530 a week in pretax paychecks. Then the government rips out a nice chunk, leaving about $400 a week for all that work. The real benefit comes in the fact that we have no expenses, as room and board are on the house, so everything I make goes straight into the bank.

Anyone who wants to make real money in Alaska is either a fisherman, which is dangerous and brutal work, or a processor who works for percentage of the catch, as opposed to hourly wage. Chris has decided he doesn't know enough about fishing to try it, which is smart. But he's hell-bent on getting a percentage processing job.

"I want to make ten grand, and I don't want to be up here forever," he tells me. I like his determination, and his logical grasp of the work involved. Most of the rookies come in expecting great wealth, failing to take into account the toll the work takes on their bodies and their psyches. "Yeah, I'll stay here a year, then I'll get twenty-five thousand," they always start out, not realizing that people who've been here a year without a break have usually gone half-mad. Then they start talking about all the wonderful things they're going to buy. Depending on who they are, these things range from bags of cocaine to brand new sport-utility vehicles. Then, two weeks later, when reality has set in, they're in the clinic complaining that they have carpal tunnel syndrome so they can get a medical and a free trip home.

Chris is different. He's only nineteen, but he has a better grasp of reality than most of the older people I'm working with.

"You mind if I take off for an hour and see if I can find another ship that's hiring?"

"Go ahead."

This becomes a daily event. Whenever there is nothing to do, Chris is off to find a better job. In the hopes that he'll find one for me too, I let him go.

One afternoon, I see Brian walking off the ship with a duffel bag. "Gonna catch my plane," he tells me. "My knee. It just gave out."

"I hate when that happens."

Later, one of the girls in the office tells me that Brian's parents had called the company insisting that they send Brian home immediately. He had been calling them every day, collect, from the satellite phone, and they had just received a $4,000 phone bill. The "nice things" he wound up paying for were six hours worth of long distance conversation.

Chris returned from his daily mission. "There's a ship leaving," he tells me. "Paying percentage. They need two more processors for a three-trip contract. They're leaving in two hours. Wanna go?"

I mull over this career decision for a second or so. "Let's do it."

I head down to my bunk, shove all my possessions into a duffel bag, and go up to the front office to tell them where to forward my paycheck. There are no tears of farewell. I've already lasted significantly longer than most processors.

We take a taxi out to the *Royal Golden*, where Chris has found us a job, and I see the boy has done well. The ship is spotless—no rust anywhere, no creaky doors, no water on the floor. The office staff actually wants me to do paperwork, and there's a real check of my ID and a few questions. In Alaska, this is akin to the three-month background check usually associated with getting government jobs. I am hopeful that they don't go so far as checking my name with the police, who are expecting me to show up any day for community service. And as the *Royal Golden* heads out to sea, I stand on the deck, watching Dutch Harbor get smaller, and imagine frustrated cops standing on the docks cursing. So long, *suckahs*.

I haven't been out to sea in a while, and the first thing I remember is that I get viciously seasick. I spend the first two days of the first trip rushing back and forth to the bathroom and vomiting. The other thing I realize is that if you are being paid a percentage of the catch, hours mean nothing. You don't punch in and out, and the company isn't saving money by having you not work. So everyone has to be busy all the time. Between bouts of vomiting, I'm expected to pitch in and clean the galley, scrub pots, clean the processing room, move boxes in the freezer, and any other menial job that comes up. After about two days of this, I finally just blow off a shift and crawl back in bed, where the supervisor finds me.

"What're you doing in bed?" he asks.

"I keep puking. I just needed a few hours of rest."

"Fuck," he says, shaking his head, obviously disgusted with me. He walks out. I can take his disgust at this point. I just need to be left alone.

Chris doesn't get seasick, and soon becomes the golden boy of the new-hires. He attacks every menial job eagerly and is soon sitting at the supervisor's table at the mess. The supervisors look at me each time I walk by, and I know the look. It's that "He's not going to work out" look I often gave the new-hires at Rayford.

By the third day, we get out to the fishing grounds, and my body is adjusting to the rolling of the ship. I'm starting to feel a little better, and I try pitching in more, try to sound enthusiastic when given an assignment. When the fish start coming in, I spend my first shift on the slime lime, packing mackerel, but it's difficult to distinguish yourself doing tedious, repetitive work. A few days go by, and I'm still getting the looks.

I'm sent to the slime line to process. Processing at sea is essentially the same as processing on land, except that the *Royal Golden* is a fishing boat and we catch the fish we process. For each trip, we have orders to fill. On this trip, Korean buyers have asked us to catch mackerel and pack them in-the-round, or uncut, which is easy work. The hard part of processing is the gutting, which involves grasping the fish and working with it, wearing out your hands. But with the mackerel, we have no gutting. We merely have to catch the mackerel, then fit them into small trays and stuff the trays into a blast freezer. After three hours, the trays are broken out, slammed against a metal shield that dislodges the frozen mackerel in neat squares, and they are packed into cases. The cases are then banded and sent down into a freezer.

I'm on the slime line for about an hour on my second processing day when I get a tap on the shoulder, and the supervisor tells me he's got a job for me. That's usually not a good sign, but I'd rather do anything than stand still and process. He takes me to a room with stainless steel walls, and a big hole in one wall where a giant funnel leads to a conveyor belt.

The supervisor hands me a shovel. "When the fish come in," he tells me, "push 'em onto the belt."

"Okay."

He points at a red button on the wall. "That's the panic button."

"Panic button?"

"Yeah. Try not to use it."

"Okay." He leaves. I'm off the slime line. Back here, in this nice quiet room by myself, I've got the best of everything. It's almost quiet, I've got some privacy, I can even sing to myself if I want. And all I have to do is push fish onto a conveyor belt and not use the panic button.

I look around the room. On every wall there is a panic button. People must panic a lot down here.

Then a hydraulic motor slides the roof of the room back, and I'm looking at the sky. I can hear the deck crew shouting to each other and I tilt my head back to feel the rain in my face. I see darkening clouds, and I'm admiring the purple hue of the sunset when a large net is swung directly over me by a giant crane, blocking out the sky. The net is full of fish.

One of the fishermen on deck sticks his head over my hole. "Stand in the corner!" he screams.

"WHAT?" I can barely hear him over the noise of the hydraulic motors and the sea.

"Stand in the goddamned corner! Get out of the way!"

I realize what is going on just in time. I leap back into the corner just as the net opens and dumps several tons of fish into the room. I am suddenly chest-high in fish, and most of them are still moving. Then the roof closes again and I am in a dark room full of live fish.

There is nothing else to do, so I start pushing the fish toward the hole.

After about twenty minutes of pushing, I've got the fish level down to my waist. The fish down this low are mostly dead, killed by the fall or the pressure of having tons of fish on top of them for so long. This, combined with the fact that I can now move most of my lower body, permits me to get my legs into the shoveling and the second half goes easy. By the time I am walking around picking up the last of the fish off the floor and tossing them through the hole in the wall, I'm feeling pretty pleased with myself.

Then the roof slides back again. I leap back into the corner.

Another netful of live fish, still flipping seawater off their tails as they crash into the room. This time, the shipment comes up to my neck. I can barely move, and I can feel the pressure of all the fish making it hard to breathe. I suddenly see the value of a panic button, though I can't imagine how you could use it if you actually needed it, as your arms would be under fish level.

I try wriggling my way up, and after about three or four minutes, I'm on top of the pile of fish, gasping for air. Some guy sticks his head through the hole and yells, "Hey are you gonna push these fish through or what?"

I sit on the big pile of fish and start pushing them through with my feet. This works pretty well for a while, but my legs get too tired to move after a bit so I find the shovel, stand on a pile of fish, and start shoveling. This goes okay until my back gets tired, so I sit down and use my feet again.

The guy sticks his head through the hole. "Slow down, man, you're killing us."

Okay, that's nice. I can slow down for a bit. I realize there are people sorting the fish on the other side of the line, and I must have been backing them up. I try to find a nice rhythm. I get enough fish out to start using the shovel, and before I know it, the fish room is empty again.

The roof comes back, the net comes into view. The fisherman looks down at me. I am panting. He laughs.

"Next load is perch. You know what that means."

I've got no idea what it means, but it doesn't sound good. It isn't. A load of bright red fish come slamming down into the bin, and every one of them has a thousand spiny splinters across its back. I try to wade into them and the red quills rip into my rain gear. I'm getting poked all over. I can't push the fish because the spines go through my gloves. I can't sit on the fish and kick them out because the spines go through my ass. I'm in a room full of needles.

Finally, I lose my temper and start slamming the fish through the hole, screaming at the top of my lungs. There's no other way to end this. After about twenty minutes, I've got enough of them out to use the shovel, so the last half goes a lot easier. When the load of perch is gone, the roof opens up and the fisherman is laughing.

"Last one before break," he tells me. "This one's mackerel."

Mackerel. Sweet, oily, smooth, unspined mackerel. Last time I was pushing mackerel, I didn't know how good I had it. I struggle with the mackerel, shoveling armloads through the hole. Fuck 'em if I'm going too fast, this is the last one before break. Let them go faster. I can feel the muscles in my arms, as well as my legs, cramping up now. When I bend over to use the shovel, my back is burning. The fucker who took me off the slime line wanted to kill me. That's what the looks meant. They tried to bury me in a fish pile, and if I lived, I'd have the most miserable job on the fucking ship. Fuckers. I love this shit. More mackerel through the hole. More, more, more. I am nearly prostrate when the last of the mackerel have gone through, and I hear the bolt on my door sliding open. I turn around and stand up straight, like I have just returned from a walk in the park. Kill me, will you.

The supervisor is looking at me. He bursts out laughing. "Those perch'll get you, won't they?"

I look down at my rain gear. I'm covered all over in red needles, like a giant red porcupine. My gloves too. I reach up to scratch my nose and nearly poke my eye out.

"Take a break," he says. "You did good."

"You smell like fish," Chris tells me in the galley. "I mean, I know we're working with fish, and most of us smell like fish, but you *really* smell like fish."

The gentle rocking of the ship doesn't bother me anymore, except when I'm trying to sip my coffee. I keep spilling it down my chin. Then I realize the ship isn't doing it, my muscles have just started freezing up. I'm banging a cup of hot coffee into my own face, and the more I try to control it, the worse it gets.

"Easy, easy," Chris says, reaching over, taking the coffee from me. "Are you all right?"

Despite myself, I'm having a fit of giggles. I'm losing it mentally too. Then my legs start to take on a life of their own, knocking up against the table. I'm losing control of my own body.

A different supervisor is walking by, sees me convulsing at the table. "You pushing just now?"

"Yeah."

"First time?"

"Yeah."

"Go take a hot shower. Miss the rest of the shift."

It's a rare order. Nobody ever gets to miss the rest of a shift, not on percentage work. Everyone is getting the same percentage, so we're all motivated to make sure each other pulls their own weight. But I don't see what function I could possibly perform now, having developed some kind of palsy. I go up the stairs to the shower.

There are six showers for 180 processors; three showers for the twelve women on board and three for the men, 168 of us. Because we are divided into two shifts of ninety, I wake up and go to work with over eighty individuals using three showers. Average shower length is about a minute. Nobody adjusts the water temperature; we just hop in, run soap over ourselves, and hop out. That was the way at Rayford too. But now I'm off shift while my group is working and the other is sleeping, and I have three showers to myself.

This is the stuff that makes life worth living. A half hour, a hot shower, the water soaking my battered muscles as I listen to the thrum of the hydraulic motors in the processing room below. I have privacy; I have heat. No one is on the other side of the shower door, waiting, for the first time in five months. I step out of the shower, and steam is coming off my skin. I crawl into my bunk and sleep, the first fully relaxed sleep of my stay on the *Royal Golden*.

It's short-lived. I wake up after about an hour, with my muscles cramping up again, only now I'm in a narrow bunk with an opposite shift worker above me. These bunks are three high, and I'm in the middle one. The more my leg cramps, the more I try to move it around to ease the pain, and the more it cramps. I can't get out of the bunk because I've only got two feet of space to work with. The pain is agonizing, and I start yelling, and the guy above me sticks his head down into my bunk.

"What the fuck's the matter with you? We're trying to sleep."

Despite the pain, I can still feel embarrassment. "You gotta help me get out of this bunk. I'm cramping up."

The guy shakes his head, disgusted, but hops down and helps me out of the bunk. He dumps me on the floor and crawls back under his covers.

I lie on the floor for a while, trying to relax my muscles. Now I have freedom of movement, it's a lot easier, and after a while, I drift off to sleep on the floor.

The supervisor comes in and taps me awake with his boot. "We need you for a kick shift," he says. "We let you off early, so we're bringing you on again early."

Kick shifts are extra half-shifts, which everyone is required to work from time to time. My turn is now. I sit up, test my legs. There's slight pain there, but I have control of them at least.

"Where you want to work?" he asks. He has a clipboard in his hands. "You did a good job pushing fish. Want to go back there?"

"Sure."

So I'm back in the fish room, with my rubber fish shovel. Now I know what to expect, I can pace myself a little better. After each load of fish, I stretch, try to relax. There is a bar in the ceiling by one of the corners and I can do a pull-up on it when the fish are coming down so that I don't get buried alive. This is obviously the bar's purpose, but no one has bothered to explain this to me. I keep an extra pair of gloves handy so I can double-glove when the perch come down and not get pricked to death. Once I learn a few tricks like this, the fish room becomes my home.

Toward the end of the two-week trip, I see myself getting out of the shower one morning and notice that I have built up pounds of muscle on my shoulders and biceps. I look like a bodybuilder. I discover the first of the fish room's benefits. The second is that no matter what else I am asked to do, it's always an improvement on what I'm doing now. The fish room is considered to be the worst job on the ship, and there's a certain status that goes along with it. Thus, when our hold is full and we are coming back into port, I am given the easiest of the off-load jobs—helping the fishermen repair nets on deck. I get to see Dutch Harbor come into view, our first look at land in sixteen days, and the misty mountains and little shacks that dot the landscape are a beautiful sight.

As with every trip, there is a crew exchange. The crew members who have finished their three-trip contract file off and say their good-byes, and we get fresh meat—new kids straight off the plane. College kids giddy with the idea of working in Alaska run around on the deck, marveling at the mountains and the giant fishing cranes, cracking jokes and struggling to pay attention as the supervisors take them through the initiation process. These kids are less than one day removed from the world, a world I realize I have all but forgotten. A world of restaurants where the customer is always right, where there are coffee shops on the corner, designer clothes, MTV, $150 sneakers, and everybody drives a car, where more than a minute in the shower every day is a reality.

I'm gonna love watching 'em squirm.

Since my hire on the *Royal Golden*, I haven't seen much of Chris, but the supervisors have taken to him, just as I did at Rayford. He is offered the job of freezer foreman for the second trip, and asks to have me on his crew. This means that I get moved out of the fish room and the job is given to one of the new kids.

The freezer is money for nothing, a walk in the park. All I have to do is stand in a giant freezer hold, wearing something that looks like a space suit without the glass face mask, and stack boxes that come down off a conveyor belt. Chris and I are alone down here in this hold, which is quiet except for the humming of the refrigeration unit and the *whoosh* of a box coming down the belt every five seconds. We have some good conversations about everyone in Alaska's favorite topic—what we're going to do with all the money when we get home.

"I'm going to start my own business," he tells me. "I figure about ten thousand ought to get it going."

"Doing what?"

"I don't know."

"Sounds like a winner."

"What are you going to do, smart guy?"

"No idea."

"Sounds well thought out."

"Fuck you."

"Fuck you."

I figure Bill Gates was having conversations like this before he came up with Microsoft.

To kill the monotony of walking back and forth with boxes, Chris and I invent a game. We put our faces over the slide in front of the conveyor belt and hold them there for as long as we can, pulling away at the last second before a sixty-pound box of frozen fish creams us. The one who can leave his face over the belt for the longest wins.

It's only a matter of a few boxes before the inevitable happens. Chris is nearly knocked unconscious, and I get a bloody nose. Boxes keep coming down the slide as we are trying to reorient ourselves. The boxes roll along the belt, then plop off onto the freezer room floor, piling up at the end of the belt.

"Oh God, my head," Chris groans.

I think I've broken my nose, but it doesn't hurt that much, and I get up and move around. Chris has been pasted. He tries to stand but the room is spinning on him, and being in a hold of a ship that actually is spinning doesn't help. He lets loose some vomit on the floor, which freezes into a rock.

I try grabbing a box or two and stacking them myself while Chris gets his bearings, but he's not coming around. A few more boxes *whoosh* down the slide and along the belt while I watch him try to stand again.

"I'm going to put you up on the lift. Make 'em stop the line for a minute. We'll say it was an accident."

"No. They'll cut my percentage." He tries to stand again.

Whoosh. Whoosh. The pile of boxes at the end of the belt is getting out of hand. We'd better say something soon or the supervisors are going to be pissed.

"I'll be okay, I just need a minute," Chris groans.

I grab a box, and run over and stack it, then another, working double time. I jog back and forth with the boxes, trying to take two at a time. There is ice on the floor and the boxes are heavy and hard to grab. We start hitting some rough sea and the floor of the freezer hold starts moving up and down, sliding the boxes around. It's hard to walk, let alone jog, but I do my best with it. After a few minutes, there are only a few boxes lying by the belt, and I kick them all, soccer style, over to the stack while carrying two others.

Chris is able to stand by this point. He watches me work for the rest of the hour and we go up at break time and tell the supervisor that he slipped and fell.

"How come you got a bloody nose?" the super asks me suspiciously.

"I fell too."

"Were you two fighting down there?"

"Hell, no," I say angrily enough to deflect further questions. He eyes us warily.

But Chris is screwed. If someone gets legitimately injured on a percentage boat, he's dead weight. The company prefers that anyone with a legitimate injury stay in their cabin, so that the other working crew members can't lay eyes on his uselessness. Injured people are required to eat at their own mealtimes, after the working crew has eaten, effectively ostracized from the bunch. The purpose of this is to discourage people from claiming an injury. The company has the hope that no matter how badly you hurt yourself, you carry on with it and don't let them know.

Quitters receive the same treatment, but almost nobody quits outright. Quitting is usually accompanied by claims of a dozen suddenly remembered ailments, blown knees, carpal tunnel syndrome, claims that a relative has been in a car accident, and on and on. Because no one is ever 100 percent positive if a claim is false, it's assumed that anyone with an injury claim is lying. So Chris, who was a great worker with a real concussion, is treated like dirt. Now he has to spend a week and a half sitting in a bunk room, waiting for the hold to fill up so he can go home.

For my sins, they send me down a new kid to help in the freezer.

I'm upset about losing a friend who I enjoyed working with, but I'm even more upset after meeting William. He's the whiniest kid I've ever met. Some people should never have come to Alaska in the first place. He doesn't care about anything but going home.

He's been on the boat for less than a week and already the supervisors have moved him to three different jobs, trying to find something for him that he won't whine about. He's whined about all of them. Give the supervisors credit. They do try to find a niche where everyone works their best; but with William, they've given up. The kid isn't going to work out, and they've tossed him down in the freezer with me so they won't have to look at him.

I take it as a challenge. I'm gonna turn this kid around. By the time I'm through with him, he's going to love these boxes, he's going to protest when they tell him to take a break. This is my freezer and down here we work or we freeze.

William has the unusual habit of sitting down between boxes, which seems to me like a huge waste of energy, as the boxes for each of us come only ten seconds apart. The result is the same as doing a squat thrust between each box. This is his personal form of protest, sitting, his way of saying he wants a break; but all it is accomplishing is making him need one even more.

"Stop sitting down between boxes," I tell him in my gruffest voice. "You're wasting your energy."

"You're not a supervisor," he sulks, shuffling over, stacking a box, then shuffling back and sitting down for three seconds before his next box comes down the chute.

"You're making yourself tired," I say. "You need to stay on your feet."

"Who're you? You're just a guy who works in a freezer. You're not a supervisor." He sits down again.

This goes on for about fifteen minutes, and he eventually runs out of what little energy he has. I take a box, and when it's his turn to take a box, he just lets it fall off the end of the belt.

"That's your box," I tell him, getting my own.

"I just need to sit down."

I stack my box and another of his falls. "Dickhead, pick up

your boxes! This isn't break time!" I've never worked with anyone before who has achieved his level of apathy. I'm not giving up. He's my personal experiment, and I'm going to turn him into a finely tuned, box-stacking machine. "Get your box!"

He sits and stares. I walk over to him and put my face in his face. "Get your box! Get your box! Get your box! Get your box! GET YOUR GODDAMNED MOTHERFUCKING PIECE OF SHIT BOX!"

He gets up and wordlessly gets back to work.

I see a glimmer of hope. I am the warm-hearted but tough drill sergeant and he is the hopeless private who I am going to whip into shape.

"How's pussy-boy?" one of the supervisors asks me when we come up from the freezer.

"He's great. He kicks ass. He's a regular fireball."

"You're kidding, right?"

"No. He's a good worker."

The supervisor eyes me warily again. He no longer believes anything I say. He shrugs "Okay, you keep him."

"Suits me."

The next shift is no different, perhaps even worse. William sits down between boxes and starts letting the boxes drop onto the floor after about an hour. I don't have the energy to scream at him again, so I try reasoning.

"Look, you're stuck here," I tell him. "You signed a contract. It's only nine weeks. Nine weeks of your life, all you gotta do is stack boxes. Then you go home with five thousand dollars. Think about the five thousand dollars, man. Think what you're going to do with all that money."

He sits and stares.

"Where do you live?" I ask him.

"Oregon."

"Got your own place?"

"I live with my dad. He's an asshole. He keeps throwing me out."

"Five grand, man. You don't have to take any of his shit anymore. Five grand, you get your own place. Five thousand dollars. You could have women eating out of your hand. Five grand. Think of it." I'm getting myself pumped up, imagining all the fun I'm going to have when I get out of this shithole freezer. William isn't talking, so I tell him about my plans, which come to me as I talk. I'm going to put down a security deposit on a beautiful inner city apartment and buy furniture and get cable hooked up legally and sit on my ass all day on my new leather couch and watch bad television. I'm going to take beautiful women out on dates and walk along the river with them. I'm going to find a job, a nice job that I can stand where I work with people I like, doing something satisfying, something that makes me feel good about myself, while I'm making enough money to pay my bills and maybe save a little extra every month. If you've got five thousand dollars, you have the time to actually look for something decent. I tell William all this and realize that I'm becoming carried away with my own enthusiasm.

"I quit," says William.

"Fucker quit," I tell the super.

"He what?"

"He quit. He wants to go sit in his cabin until we get back to Dutch."

"I thought you said he was a fireball."

"He started to show some promise. I might have exaggerated."

"No shit." The supervisor rolls his eyes. "I'm gonna send you down someone else. I don't want his head smashed in and I don't want you to make him quit."

"Fine. Give me someone worth a shit this time."

"I know what I'm gonna do with my cash," Little Jimmy tells me. Little Jimmy is my new partner, a hyperactive, energetic non-stop-talker who is everything William was not. He's been on the *Royal Golden* for seven contracts, which is nearly a year of his life. He's covered in tattoos and he seems to have a permanent nosebleed, which others tell me is from cocaine binges between each of his contracts. The bleeding nose makes him a bad bet to put around uncovered fish, so he pulls freezer duty, which he doesn't like.

"I'm gonna take it to Tahoe and put it all on one round of roulette. Double or nothing, baby."

I cringe to hear this. I'm not exactly the world's best money manager, but having spent four months at Rayford and two weeks in a fish room, the thought of watching a ball bearing bounce into a red hole making me broke again is almost heartbreaking.

"Don't do that," I plead.

He shrugs, as if I have a better plan. "Well, what're you gonna do?"

"Put a down payment on a nice apartment."

He nods wisely. "Nice apartment. Whatever. I got a plan."

"That's not a plan, you idiot."

"Hey, fuck you. What're you, my mother?"

"You're just killing yourself to give your money away to casino owners."

"And you're giving it to landlords."

I don't say anything. He's right. "I'll tell you something about money, man," he says. "You either got it or you don't. You and me, we don't got it."

I'm not sure I like being grouped in with him. I'm not down here for my next coke binge and five-minute stand at the roulette table. I'm here to make a life, start a life, get some options for a life. Put some distance between myself and the guys begging in the street.

But Little Jimmy can stack boxes like a whirlwind. It's hard for me to keep up with him as he keeps running back to the belt, and sometimes he grabs my box as well as his own.

"Once you've learned to eat shit, you realize it don't taste so bad," he says. That's a beautiful motto for life. I want to give him some advice, to set him straight about some financial management issues. Hard as he works, he should be going somewhere, building something. But he doesn't care. He has all this energy, all this commitment, and it's going to add up to nothing. He'll wind up in the same boat as William, who is upstairs lying on his fat ass reading comics, imagining the sweet homecoming when his abusive father picks him up at the airport.

"You can't throw it all away at roulette," I tell him again. "That's stupid."

"Not if I win."

"If you win you'll just play again until you lose."

"Right on. Now you understand."

It wears on me sometimes. It wears on all of us, but some days are worse than others. Some days you crawl out of bed and the rocking of the ship makes it hard to put your pants on and you just want to get back under the covers and sob. Your nerves are like raw cut flesh, screaming in pain and annoyance at any touch, any mention of your name. On days like this, toward the end of the trip, we stand in the breakfast line and stare blankly as we spoon food onto our plate, sit silently as we shovel it down. Even Little Jimmy is getting exhausted enough to be quiet. I shrug into my freezer suit as the others shrug into their rain gear. Not even the guys coming off shift are saying much.

My hands are like claws from grabbing the boxes, and every morning the muscles have to relax all over again. The first half hour is the worst, my stomach still heavy from the breakfast food, mind still numb from sleep. On days like this, and they're mostly like this now, it's good to work with Little Jimmy, with a guy who's been doing it long enough to do it blindfolded and who's always ready to pull his weight.

About an hour into the shift, I miss a lock. When we stack the boxes, we have to make the boxes on every fifth row face a different direction. This row is called a lock, and it makes the stacks more stable. If every row was stacked the same, by the time they were fifteen or sixteen high, they would be like a load of unmortared bricks, ready to tumble every time the ship took a turn. Jimmy points out the lock to me, and I have to scramble to replace it. Then I miss the next one, and he gets pissed.

"Come on, man," he yells, annoyed. I make a mental note to keep counting the stacks, but my mind keeps wandering. In my determination not to miss a lock, I put one in on the fourth row.

"What the fuck's the matter with you?" he starts screaming. This seems like an overreaction to me, so I tell him to calm down.

"What do you mean calm down. Can't you count to five?"

"Fuck you. Get over it."

"You're a fucking retard."

I'm about to walk over and pound him when the conveyor belt shuts off. We look at each other, both thinking the same thing. Mechanical failure. Every time something shuts off, we all have the same glimmer of hope. Mechanical failures mean unscheduled break time.

Usually when stuff shuts off, it's just a minute, and then it starts back up again. Of course, we don't want the thing permanently damaged because then we don't make as much money. But the odd twenty-minute break now and again is a rare blessing.

The lift door opens and a super sticks his head down. "You guys come up here," he says. "Break time."

We look at each other and smile, high five. Some days you just can't handle it. You just weren't meant to be there. Some days you get a little relief. We sit in the galley eating cookies and chatting for four hours while electricians walk back and forth and curse. Some of us even put our heads down on the Formica tables and nap. When we hear the hydraulics start up again, there's only about an hour of our shift left.

"We lost a lot of time, so we have to work a kick shift to make up for it," the supervisors announce. But no one cares. We got a break. We got a little time off when we weren't expecting it. It was beautiful.

The hold is full, and we're heading back into Dutch, and my contract is over. Your last trip, they don't make you off-load. They use the new kids coming aboard to replace you to do that. The idea is that after nine weeks at sea, it's hard for you to keep your mind on your work if you're about to get a check for five grand and a plane ticket, so they just bid you farewell.

One day out of Dutch Harbor, the super tells us there is a meeting for all the personnel who got hired on in Dutch.

"Let me get right to the point," he tells us. "The company isn't paying your plane tickets home."

We all stare at him in shock. The company has only agreed to pay the plane tickets of the people it flew up here. As we all flew up with a different company, they're under no obligations to pay our ticket back to Seattle. So my five grand has become thirty-five hundred.

"I know it's wrong, because you guys all did a great job," he's telling us, but the rest is just corporate blather. It wasn't his decision, we all know. If there's no legal obligation, there's no obligation. It's the way the world works.

I shrug. It's over. I lasted. I wanted five grand, but I'll take what I got.

"We're still going to put you up in a bunkhouse," he tells us. This is a tradition, apparently, to let the guys who have finished their contracts party it up the day before they catch their plane. We get a bunkhouse to ourselves, and we're on our own to get liquor and anything else we can find.

We're too tired to argue. What good would it do, anyway? We shuffle out of the galley for a final shift of cleanup.

I'm packing my stuff, a duffel bag full of dirty and ragged clothes, and a Mexican guy I've been bunking with for three weeks comes in, excited, and motions for me to come with him. I follow him up onto deck, out into the sunlight, where the processors are hardly ever allowed. He points off the bow.

There, I see a whale's tail splashing the surf. It's enormous. It seems like the tail alone is about the size of this ship. The ship follows alongside for a while, and I see fountains of seawater come out his blow hole. The Mexican, who I've never talked to before, and I, stand there and watch the whale for a few minutes until the ship turns off. There was no reason for him to come and get me. He could have just stood here and watched the whale on his own. Sometimes people are like that.

On the other side, Dutch Harbor comes into view. I'm going home.

The bunkhouse is a squalid shack on the wrong side of a town that doesn't have a right one. The road leading up to it is frozen mud, which would be a rough ride even for a tank. But there are beds. Real beds.

I sit on the side of my bed, in a room with five others, and the room feels like it's moving. After weeks at sea, my body has become so used to continual movement that it makes me slightly queasy to be completely still. Landsickness. I stand up to go to the bathroom and the level, stationary floor catches me off guard, and I have to walk slowly.

When I come back to the room, there is a fisherman there, talking to the guys lying on the beds. "You can ask him," one of them tells the fisherman, pointing at me. "But none of us are interested."

"You want a job?" the fisherman asks me.

"I'm worn out," I tell him, but just out of interest, I ask to find out what I'm missing.

"Crab fishing. Five thousand, two weeks. Whaddya say?"

I look around the room. All these guys have said no already. But five thousand for two more weeks? Then I look at my bed. It looks good.

"What boat?"

"The *Killoran*."

I've never heard of it. Don't know why I asked, but now he thinks I'm interested. "I don't know how to crab fish," I tell him. "Never done it before."

"That's okay. We just need one more deckhand. We'll train."

They'll train. In a classified ad, that's English for: we suck to work for, and nobody with any experience will hire on with us. Who knows, maybe up here it's different.

"What happened to the last guy?"

"He quit. Couldn't take it."

My hands are moving to grab my stuff. I'm looking at them, as if they have lives of their own. My hands have already decided to go. I'm still burning about having to pay my own plane ticket back, and this will make up for it.

"Let's do it," I say.

After four days on the *Killoran*, I realize I have finally done it. I've found the worst fucking job in the world.

I've managed to find something that combines everything unpleasant in life with a low paycheck. This is going to be a low paycheck because I signed on for a percentage, and we're not catching any crab. Up until a few days ago, the Bering Sea was full of opilio crab, so I'm told. But the season has been dragging on for a few months and the waters are getting fished out.

The horrible thing about crab fishing is that you have to work just as hard to catch one crab as you do to catch a thousand. There are about fifty or so large steel frames covered with netting called crab pots on our deck. These crab pots, which are about seven feet by seven feet, weigh hundreds of pounds. We slide them across the deck up against a device called a dog, which has metal clamps that hold it fast while we put a bait can inside. Then we hit a hydraulic switch on the dog and the pot gets dumped to the bottom of the Bering Sea. All this gets done at breakneck speed, so that the skipper doesn't have to keep stopping the boat.

The idea, of course, is that the crab will smell the bait, crawl inside the pot, and be trapped. A few days later, we go back, pull up our pots, and pull tons of crab up onto our deck. This isn't happening. Most of our pots are nearly empty. Some of them have a few dozen crab inside, but none are full. If we were filling every pot, we could fill our hold in the two weeks I was promised, but at this rate, we're going to be out here for a month at least.

I've been royally fucked. But I'm on a crab boat 100 miles out in the Bering with four other guys. Going back isn't an option. Quitting and sitting in my cabin isn't an option. I know because I asked. Crab fishing is the option, and it isn't going well.

The first thing about crab fishing is that there are about a hundred different ways to die when you are doing it. Nobody will insure crab fishermen, I'm told, because we're simply not a good risk. Up to five percent of them get killed or injured every year, which aren't much better odds than combat. The deck is usually icy and the steel crab pots can fall on you, which is the most common way to die. Before sliding the pots, we hook them to a crane, but if the boat rocks a lot while we're moving, the crane doesn't help much. Sometimes, when the wind gets up, the pot can whip around like a seven-hundred-pound steel tetherball, looking for something to smash.

The other big danger is falling overboard. The water is cold enough to kill you in about a minute, and the seas are rocky enough to sweep you hundreds of feet from the boat in just a few seconds, making recovery impossible. Once you're in the water, you're done. And aside from losing your balance, which isn't that hard on an icy, pitching deck, there are a dozen ways to wind up in the water. (See crab pot, above.) Also, if someone accidentally hits the hydraulic switch on the dog to drop the pot while you're placing the bait cans, you go down with the pot.

Or, you can have your feet wrapped up in the buoy strings, which are the ropes attached to the buoy that identify the pot once it is in the water. The pot drags the ropes down with it, so it's a good idea to steer clear of these ropes when you're dropping pots.

Boris, the fisherman who hired me at the bunkhouse, has seen people die all these ways since becoming a fisherman three years ago. I ask him about the people.

"They were new guys," he tells me. Then, remembering how long I've been here, he hastily adds, "and they didn't listen."

I listen intently. Mostly, I listen to the skipper screaming at me, telling me what an idiot I am.

"What the fuck are you doing?" he screams over the loud-speaker from the bridge. "What the FUCK DO YOU THINK YOU'RE DOING?" I'm trying to pull crab out of the pot, where they are clinging to the net, and I know that if you pull hard, you break their legs off, which causes them to emit a poison that kills the other crab. Therefore, you have to be gentle with the little guys.

Boris, who is an experienced fisherman who knows how to deal with the skipper's outbursts, motions for me to leave the crab in the pot. "Don't worry about it," he tells me kindly. "It's just one crab. We'll get it next time we pull up the pot." He hands me the new bait can and I hook it inside the pot, jump out, and John, the engineer, hits the switch. Splash goes the pot.

I enjoy thirty seconds of rest and inactivity while the *Killoran* chugs over to the next pot. John stands on the deck with a hook, throws the hook around the buoy, which is just a big rubber ball, and reels it in. He hooks the buoy rope around a winch, which hauls in the whole line in a matter of seconds, pulling the pot up from the deep. If it goes too fast, the pot could slam into the bottom of our boat, which is not good. So this is a job for someone who knows what they're doing.

John is a little quick with the winch and the pot bumps the bottom of the *Killoran*.

"John! You fucking idiot! Watch my boat!" Despite the fact that the whole crew knows what they're doing, and works fairly well together, the skipper calls us each fucking idiots at least once an hour. As a new guy, he expects nothing from me, so I get it less than the others. I see now why the guy who quit before me "couldn't take it." Boris tells me that compared to other skippers, ours is benign.

We pull up another half-empty crab pot, dump the crab out onto the deck, shovel them down into the hold. I rebait the pot, and splash, back down it goes.

Because we work eighteen hours on and four off, I lose track of time. I have no idea how long I've been out here. I wake up sometimes in the dark and go to bed when it's light out. I'm pulling watch, which involves sitting in the bridge looking out the window, and trying to keep myself awake by seeing if I can figure a way to find the exact date.

Every one of us has to pull two hours of watch every other day, so instead of four hours of sleep we get two. Obviously, it's very difficult to stay awake when you're alone in a quiet, dark cabin and exhausted beyond words, so there's a little device that beeps every twelve minutes to wake you up. The beeping is loud, and I've been dead asleep every time it's gone off. This time I'm determined to stay awake for twelve whole minutes.

I dig around on the bridge to try to find something like a logbook that keeps records of the date. Nothing. I guess the skipper takes them to bed with him. I look at the Loran, which is some kind of navigational system in which I was given a ten second training course, and I notice that it has a date on it in the lower right hand corner. I figured I've been out here nine days. In fact, it's been sixteen.

The skipper wakes up and comes onto the bridge, tells me we're going to take it easy today. Everybody but me, that is. As I'm in charge of the simplest thing on the boat, the bait cans, I have to get a hundred or so bait cans ready while everyone else sleeps in.

I head into the freezer, where I find cod and blocks of herring, which I smash apart with a sledgehammer. I pack the pieces into the little plastic bait cans, then put the lids on. Dawn is coming and everyone else on the boat except Boris, who is pulling watch, is asleep. My fingers are frozen and seawater keeps splashing over the bow, soaking me. Herring oil runs all over the deck. Cleaning it up will be another of my jobs. I stagger around like a robot, my mind blank. I don't even think of getting back any more, or about how much longer this is going to last. I just think about the next ten minutes, and when is the next time I get to sleep.

The cook on board is a Thai named Keno who can't cook for shit, but he thinks he can. He dumps a quart of soy sauce and ginger on everything and then overheats it, so for the past two and a half weeks, I've been eating nothing but burned seafood with an Asian flavor to it, which everyone else on the boat seems to like.

We are sitting in the galley and the boat is rocking, and my shitty meal is trying to slide away from me, and I throw my fork down. "You need to learn how to fucking cook," I tell him. I get up and toss my meal in the trash, and he lunges at me.

We tussle around in the galley for a few seconds before we

are pulled apart. We all sit back down. I get a box of Ritz crackers out of the pantry and eat those instead, the powder building up in my dry mouth. Nobody looks at each other. The break ends and we pull our rain gear back on and head out onto the deck in silence.

When the last pot in the string is pulled up, the skipper says quietly over the loudspeaker, "Okay guys, clean up." It's not an order I've heard before, and I look over at John, who shrugs.

"Clean up the deck," he explains. "We're going back to Dutch Harbor."

"But the hold's not full."

"He's given up on this trip," Boris says. "The first crab we caught have been down there two weeks already. They'll be dead if we don't take them in soon. Besides, when guys start fighting, it's usually time to go back."

We're going back. Just like that, it's over.

As we head back into Dutch, the skipper takes every opportunity to tell us how disappointed he is in all of us. "I've never had a trip like this before," he says. "You guys all over each other. Fighting like a bunch of jailbirds. Just a bunch of lazy bastards. You make me sick." He goes on like this for a good while every time we have a meal. The first time, I was hurt by it, because I've pretty much poured my heart and soul into this fucking miserable job for the past three weeks; but now I just tune him out and imagine how damned good it's going to be to lie down in the bed at the Seattle Youth Hostel and get off this fucking boat and out of fucking Alaska. I'm thinking about having a beer in Pioneer Square while I watch him tell me how worthless I am.

"You don't know shit about crab fishing," he finishes.

No argument there. I'd been pretty clear about that when he hired me.

After he has gone, Boris shrugs and laughs. "He doesn't like it when we don't catch a lot of crab," he tells me. "He's a sweetheart when the pots are full."

"Fuck him."

We're pulling into Dutch, and I'm in my bunk packing my things into my duffel bag, when the skipper comes in. "You and Boris go into town for food," he tells me. "Then we're going back out tomorrow morning."

"I'm done," I tell him.

"Your contract says one shipment. We've only got half a shipment on board."

"Boris told me two weeks. I've done that and more."

"I don't know what Boris told you. You signed a contract."

Before I came aboard the *Killoran*, I signed a contract with tiny print that, characteristically, I didn't bother to read. It was longer than the Constitution. After I'd finished the first sentence, where I saw my percentage listed at one-third of one percent of our total catch, I just signed.

"Just pay me what you owe me."

"You only get half of .3 then."

"Sounds good."

"Get off my boat then," he says.

"Not till I get my check."

He turns and walks out.

An hour later, he comes back with a check—$438.

"You've got to be fucking kidding me."

"It's all there," he tells me. He's expecting this argument, and he's got a copy of the contract with him, and a copy of the check the processing company wrote him. He pulls out a calculator and some receipts. I look at the check and realize that I've also been billed for the gas that the *Killoran* has used, and the food we've eaten. After deductions, that's all I've got left.

"You charged me for the food that fucking excuse for a cook made me? If I knew I was paying, I'd have cooked it my damned self."

The skipper shrugs.

"It wasn't a good trip," Boris tells me when he sees my check. But he can't really take my side because tomorrow morning he'll be back out there again. And I can't complain to the authorities because if I stick my head in the courthouse, I'll get carted out for blowing off my community service.

I shake Boris' hand and head off to the Dutch Harbor airport.

I'm on a plane heading out of Dutch, and I can see the snow-capped mountains of Alaska below. I feel like a prisoner out of jail after a lengthy sentence, on his way back to rejoin the world.

So I got fucked, but it happens. It happens a lot. There's nobody there to stick up for you. A long time ago, before the Depression, the labor movement was a group of courageous men standing in front of armed Pinkerton Guards with nothing but an idea—that they should be treated fairly. Now it's a bunch of Italians burying each other in stadium cement. When you're fucked, you're fucked, and if you complain you're a crybaby.

That's the thing about sticking up for the poor, you can get rich doing it. Then you're not poor anymore. Then who do you stick up for?

Look at the Soviet Union, a country founded on the notion that people who work for a living should be respected, cared about. It didn't do well. Now that one social experiment is used as a cautionary tale for anyone who thinks that people who work for a living have rights. It is almost a rationale to not respect your workers, to piss on them any way you can, to promote the highly successful capitalist ideal. Hey, I think I'll keep the money for your plane ticket. Why? Because the U.S. is still around and Russia went to hell. You don't like it, go stand in a bread line in Moscow.

I'm walking through the Seattle airport, and I can see a skyline, buses, highways, women, all things I haven't laid eyes on in quite a while. I'm walking from the gate when I notice Little Jimmy coming in the other direction.

"Back to work, brother," he says, and laughs as he walks by me. But his laugh is coarse and mirthless and he doesn't wave.

I check into the Seattle Youth Hostel and enjoy a beer, the beer I have been fantasizing about for seven months. I look around at the people at the bar, a mixed crew. How many of them are happy in their work? How many of them are happy with their mates, for that matter or their apartments, or their pets? Is it all just a series of compromises, finding the best possible alternative at the time?

There's a Special Forces training center near here, and I wind up talking to a Green Beret sergeant who has just been lost in the jungle for thirteen days. He's having the beer he was fantasizing about for the last two weeks.

"I realized something about life while I was out there," he tells me, after I have told him my tale of Alaskan woe. He stares at me unsteadily through cloudy eyes as I wait for the words of wisdom. "Drinkable water."

"Drinkable water?"

"Drinkable water." He nods sagely, looking at his beer. "As long as you've got drinkable water, you don't have any real problems."

This is the kind of opiate-of-the-masses shit that's everywhere now, on bumper stickers, on little pamphlets that people used to leave for me in lieu of a tip when I was waiting tables. Somewhere there's a nineteen-year-old girl who just got pregnant or a father of three who just lost his job. They think they've got real problems, and I bet the taps in their kitchens are running fine. But I'll give this guy the benefit of the doubt. After a near-death experience, you can go around saying crap like this for a little while. He falls off his stool and they throw him out.

I chat with a girl who is a marketing rep for a company that sells beeswax. She tells me about all the uses for the product. Apparently, it's in almost everything, and she won't rest until they start making cars out of it. She has energy and enthusiasm about her job, but I know that if I meet her again a year from now, she'll be excited about her new job, which will be selling something else. "What happened with the beeswax?" I'll ask. "Oh, I found something better. Now I'm CHIEF marketing rep for a company that sells mink dung." She has the business mind-set, the ability to get excited about anything, and beeswax is just the focus of today's enthusiasm. The important thing is her position in the company.

I wish I could have that blinders-on approach to my work. It would make everything so much easier. Just go to work, work, and go home; and it doesn't matter what you spend the day doing, as long as you're moving up in the company. Making cars, selling beeswax, gassing Jews. A job's a job.

That's how you move up in the world.

Maybe I'll give it a try.

The Internet-Brainwashing Death Ray

Back in the world, with money.

While I was away, it seems the entire world has changed. The Internet has saved us all. When I went to Alaska, there were poor people, unemployed people, people stuck in dead-end jobs. Now everyone is running their own booming Internet business.

I learn this while I'm on a date, dating being something I can actually afford to do now, at least for a little while. This girl has a job managing a website that provides advice for men who want to go out on dates, and she is the female voice. She writes articles about what kinds of flowers to get, where to go, how to make the woman feel comfortable, what current movies are a good choice—all basically common sense advice for people who don't have any of their own. The website is getting thousands of hits a day, making millions of dollars, and shares of it are on the stock market, where their value is soaring.

People are actually investing in a website that tells them what to do on a date. The old notions of investment have gone out the window, along with courteous service, and our ability to make ships and cars. It is no longer necessary to have skills or materials to become a millionaire. Now you can just type some clichéd advice into your computer and have people pay you to look at it.

I try not to sound disrespectful as I ask her questions about her job. I certainly don't want to make her uncomfortable, as I'm in the presence of a dating expert. I ask her where she gets the information she dispenses. She must be going out on a nightly basis to be as well informed as she is.

"Actually, I hardly ever go out," she tells me, without a sense of irony. Maybe she's just telling me this so I won't think she's a slut, or maybe in order to be an Internet expert, one doesn't even need knowledge of the subject of their expertise. This is marvelous. A whole new wave of business, lacking function, skill, and wisdom. Brave New World, here we come.

"So what type of movie *would* you like to see," I ask her.

"I don't care. It's really up to you."

I go out on another date with another girl who wants to become a photographer.

"First I need equipment," she tells me.

I have a friend who is trying to sell a boatload of used camera equipment, and I mention it to her.

"Not that type of equipment. I need a computer. To get on the web."

"You want to buy camera equipment off the web?" This seems rational enough, but my friend's prices are dirt cheap, as I suspect much of his merchandise was discovered in an unsuspecting neighbor's home.

"No," she explains, as if I'm a slow learner. "I want to sell my photos on the web."

"So you already have camera equipment?"

"Not yet. But first I need a computer."

What's happened to people while I was gone for a few short months? When I was up in Alaska, did I miss the Internet-Brainwashing Death Ray that has apparently affected every-one's rational thought processes? Don't photographers need camera equipment BEFORE they can sell photographs? Don't people who get paid for advice need to know what they're talk-ing about? Nope, not anymore. The Internet has changed everything.

Determined not to be the last one on my block to be a million-aire, I start looking into this Internet thing. What we have here is basically a phone line that sends pictures, and I'm initially at a loss to understand why this will change the fortunes of every-one who uses it. But the advice-columnist girl explains that these pictures can show advertising, and companies will pay you to simply have a website that people will visit. So, I wonder to myself, what kind of website will people visit? The obvious choice is one with a lot of naked women, but that option, I find out, has already been taken. By about eight million people. The fierce competition here raises questions of its own that are rele-vant to the whole computer craze.

Who are these women? If you added up all the porn sites offering thousands of pornographic images, you've got pretty much the entire female population of the United States. Is that how the Internet is changing the economy, by enabling every-one to earn extra cash as a porn star? There's got to be more to it.

Over the next few weeks, I learn a little about the Internet, and find that it's not that different from anything else in the working world. Real money on the Internet moves in tight circles, just as it does in the trucking industry or banking. The companies that own the sites that get a lot of hits are big companies to start with, and they get paid a lot for their advertising, just as the networks get a lot for airing Super Bowl commercials. Therefore, the Internet is making a ton of money for large companies by providing people with the opportunity to do things like go shopping or buy airline tickets without leaving their houses. The only way the lives of regular people are changed is that we can now order T-shirts and have the mailman bring them to us rather than spend a few hours trying to park at the mall.

What amazes me about this is that everyone thinks their future is somehow tied up in a series of picture-sending telephone wires. The photographer girl thinks this is the most important step she can take in starting a photography business. The advertising for the Internet itself seems to be entirely word-of-mouth, and incredibly effective. Everyone, no matter what kind of business they have, now has to be on-line. Corporate restaurants, car washes, dog trainers, movie theaters, all advertise on-line. There are people who think it is easier to boot up a computer, wait five minutes, and start typing, than to open a newspaper and find out what's playing at a local theater. I know because I went to a movie with one of them. Yet again, I was wondering if there was something here that I just didn't get.

This is the computer industry we're talking about, the same industry that boomed in the eighties and put the nerds down the street on the cover of national magazines as if they were heroes and saints, helping someone other than themselves. The computer industry has always had a veneer of selflessness about it, as if the developments of that industry somehow benefit society, as if Bill Gates and Michael Dell are volunteer workers in a homeless soup kitchen. These are the role models of today, the cutting edge minds, the out-of-the-box thinkers. The same people who nearly got caught with their pants down by the end of the century.

Granted, it's nice to have on-line databases. If I needed a kidney, it'd be nice if there was a place I could visit immediately that would tell me if a match was available. It's nice to be able to find old girlfriends' phone numbers in the middle of the night when I'm drunk and reminiscing. It's good to be able to find a part for a car that most mechanics just laugh at. And the global porn network is a nice touch. But to suggest that this is changing all our lives is just a plain lie. Take a look outside. The homeless are still there.

So fuck the computer industry. I'm running out of my Alaska money and I'm going back to work.

I'm as sick of work as the next guy, but I'm still practical enough to recognize the need for it. Without work, where would all the new breed of millionaires that I read about in *Time* Magazine get their dry cleaning done? Who would fix their cars? Who would strip for them when they unload their trophy wives for the evening and go out for a night on the town? Us, the un-united workers of the world. I get the newspaper and dig through the classifieds.

It's the same old crap. "CAREER OPPORTUNITY!!!" screams an ad for a $6.25 an hour warehouse clerk. They mention that they drug test. Who are they kidding? They're discouraging their target market. Who but a crack head would want an opportunity like that? Opportunity, my ass. Why is it so difficult for the people who write these ads to present their jobs in a realistic and readable fashion? Why am I always looking at classifieds that say "FUN EXCITING PLACE TO WORK" and show up to see a bunch of desk jockeys a blink away from quitting, or suicide.

All the ads are like this. There's an ad that reads "NO MULTI-LEVEL MARKETING OR COLD CALLING SALES" for a company that, a friend of mine who applied there informs me, sticks you at a desk to do cold calling, only you're not supposed to actually sell anything to the people; you get the lead for the salesman. Therefore, they've made an end run around the phrase "no cold calling sales." How brilliant. How delighted are the people going to be when they show up, fill out an application, get hired, and find out that the company they've just joined has, instead of providing them with a job they might want, carefully worded its ad to get through a verbal loophole? Then the people quit after a day, a day they've wasted when they could have been looking for something worthwhile. Does this benefit the company? Perhaps. With this endless supply of new marketing companies, a lot of them have a workforce that is expected only to last until they figure out they've been duped. If the new-hires work at the phones one morning, that's fine for the marketers. The next morning they've got a new batch. And none of these people even show up to pick up their nineteen dollar paychecks, so they have a labor force every morning that's on the house.

And at the warehouse, do the people working there, where nine employees have quit on them in the past four months, honestly think they're providing people with a wonderful opportunity? THEY work there, for God's sake; they know they're lying. Who gets excited about working in a warehouse? Would the quality of applicants really be any different if their ad said: "Just Fired From Your Last Job For Calling In Sick With A Hangover Three Times In Two Weeks? Come down to our warehouse and do the same to us—$6.25 an hour for lifting heavy boxes all day." I think not.

There's an ad in there for a fish cutter, but I pass over it. After my experience in Scarsdale, I've had enough of the political, cutthroat world of fish cutting, and after my experience in Alaska, I've had enough of seafood in general. There are ads for movers, truck drivers, and restaurant managers, all things I'm drawn to because I wouldn't have to start from scratch. But at the bottom of the page, there is an ad for a temporary service. "TRY SOMETHING DIFFERENT," it beckons.

Just what I'm looking for.

In these "prosperous" times of low unemployment, temp services are the largest employers in the country. This means that, while more jobs are available, fewer and fewer people have health benefits, sick days, or job stability.

Manpower Inc., which sometime during the last decade overtook General Motors as the largest single employer in the nation, does nothing but tell people where to go to work. All this huge corporation does is shuffle papers around and take a sizeable chunk of millions of individuals' paychecks. At least General Motors makes cars.

But, to their credit, they do get people working. They offer, as I discover, hundreds of different positions—everything from warehouse work to skilled medical positions, from truck driver to office worker. I've had enough of the physical grind lately, so I opt for office work. They give me a typing test, in which I do fairly well, or so I think, and then they ask me which of the two jobs that I've qualified for would I like the most: stuffing envelopes or unloading trucks.

"What does stuffing envelopes entail?" It sounds like an intriguing line of work, and I've never done it before. Truck unloading is old hat.

"You stuff envelopes."

"In an office?"

"Yes."

"With a coffee-maker?" It's always been a dream of mine to work near a coffee-maker.

The girl sighs. "I'm going to send you to the hotel." I guess I'm not the envelope-stuffing type. So I'm given a slip of paper and sent down to the Ramada Inn, where some fellow is putting on an art show and needs help unloading his truck. This is all rush-rush, because the people who call the agency for help usually do so at the last minute, when someone calls in sick. So I get down there and ask for the guy in charge of the art show, whose name happens to be Art.

Art is a merry, balding fellow who has been unloading a twenty-four-foot truck by himself since six o'clock that morning, and is just delighted to see me. That's always nice. And, it turns out, the work isn't difficult. The paintings, which are manufactured prints, are fairly light, and we just have to carry hundreds of them into a huge showroom and "set them up," which means laying them out on folding card tables. This has to be finished by 11:30, when the art show starts, and we've got about two hours to finish up an hour's worth of work.

Art is affable and easy to work with, and for the first time in years, I'm actually enjoying being at work. He enjoys his job, which is driving around the country in a rental truck selling prints at shows like this one. It's his own business, and business has been good lately. His wife usually comes along, he explains, but she got held back a day at the last place and he's making do without her for a few days.

"She doesn't trust me around the ladies," he tells me with a wink. "Time to have some fun."

I laugh. Just a harmless joke from a guy who's been married a while.

Or so I think. The employment agency sends along three

attractive young women to help with the selling, and within an hour, Art has hit on every one of them. I've been given a staple gun to adjust the frames for people who request it, and I sit in the back and listen to them talk about him.

"It's a shame, isn't it, his wife passing away suddenly like that," one of the girls tells me. I nod sympathetically. I see him engaged in rapt conversation with a pretty young woman who has come to look at some paintings. She laughs flirtatiously, writes something down on a piece of paper, and hands it to him, then leaves with a baby in a stroller, and three paintings, which I carry to her car.

"It's a shame isn't it?" she tells me as I'm walking with her through the parking lot. "The Special Forces just getting rid of him like that."

"That's the government for you."

I spend the day hooking frames together, chatting with people, and wandering around the hotel. This is the easiest day of work I've had in a while, and at eight in the evening, Art comes up to me and asks if I can work tomorrow.

"Fine with me, if the agency says so."

"I've already asked them. They said yes."

"Fine with me, then."

"I've decided to stay here for a second day. So we won't have to load everything back in the truck. You can just take a room at the hotel here, if you like, on me."

"I only live about six miles away."

"This'll save you gas money." He laughs. I shrug. We lock everything up, and as I'm going to my room, the woman who had the baby stroller shows up looking for Art. She's put on some makeup and a nice revealing skirt. I tell her where to find him, then retire to my room to watch cable. I've worked twelve hours, made nearly $100, and haven't really done anything. I could get used to this.

"You're a good worker," Art tells me the next day while I'm punching a frame together. "I need somebody like you full time. I'm looking to expand."

"Don't you go on the road?"

"I need a partner," he tells me. "For a two-thousand-dollar investment, you could get your own truck. You could operate one area while I take another."

This seems like easy and enjoyable work, but I'm skeptical about the $2,000.

"I paid $4,000 for the franchise," he explains. "You could have half. I'll get everything ready for you. Look, do you know how much money I made yesterday? Thirty-two hundred dollars! That's your investment back in one day!"

"I'll think about it." Art wanders off to chat with a pair of college girls looking for a print for their dorm room. They don't hand him any phone numbers, but they do walk off with armloads of prints. Nobody can say no to this man.

One of the girls who has shown up to sell tells me, "Art just offered me a partnership. He thinks I do really good work."

"Oh, really. Did he ask you for $2,000?"

"He said I'd have to invest something. We're going to lunch to talk about it."

Art comes over. "Me and Janine are heading off to lunch." He grabs my shoulder and looks at me with sincerity. "I trust you. You're in charge until I come back."

"Sure." We're pretty slow right now. Just a few housewives wandering around, looking at prints. Art walks off with Janine, putting his hand gently around her waist as they leave.

About half an hour later, a harried blond woman comes in wearing jeans and a T-shirt. "Is Art around?"

This guy's been in town one day and he's got more women looking for him than I've had in years.

"He went to lunch," I tell her.

"Let me guess. With a girl."

I quickly realize that this is his wife. "I didn't see. He just left."

"Bullshit." She comes around the table and introduces herself, then scoops up all the cash in the drawer. "You can't trust that bastard with money, either," she says, as she storms out.

So this isn't turning out to be my dream job either. Instead of having a few nice easy hours selling paintings with a jovial boss, I now find myself caught in the middle of a soap opera. Art, who has "gone to lunch," doesn't return for five hours. His wife doesn't come back either. So their entire business is left in the hands of a guy from the temp service he has known for a day.

Around six o'clock, when I'm wondering if I should just close up shop and load everything back into the truck, Art and Janine come back, looking a bit disheveled but holding hands.

"Your wife came by," I tell him. I wonder if he's spent the afternoon telling Janine about his wife's battle with terminal cancer, or the time Charlie had him surrounded and all he had was a penknife and a box of matches. But the news of her arrival doesn't seem to surprise Janine. Art is the one who gets upset.

"Did the bitch take my money?"

"Yup."

"Where'd she go?"

"I don't know."

Art storms off, leaving Janine there with me for another two hours. I have no idea what I'm supposed to do with all this artwork. I realize I don't have keys to load it into the truck, and if I didn't have to get his signature on my temp time card, I'd just go home right now.

Janine starts telling me about what a wonderful guy Art is. Perhaps she's convinced he was the first man to walk on the moon.

"Listen. I'll be at the bar if Mr. Wonderful comes back. At nine thirty, I'm going home." I go to the hotel bar and order a beer, and after a few minutes, Janine comes in and joins me.

"I know what you're thinking," she tells me. I'm thinking about whether or not I'm going to get paid because my employer has disappeared without signing my time card. "Most people are so boring. I know he's full of shit, but he's not dull."

He's not dull. That's great. This is a guy who would have taken $2,000 from either one of us and jetted off without a word. This is the type of person I've become sick of over the past few years, the smooth talker who wants something from you and takes it the minute you let your guard down. These are the people we need to guard ourselves against, the encroaching evil that feeds on what's left of us after a career of failure and disappointment, and this girl sees him as entertainment.

She touches my leg. Maybe I'm entertainment too. "Listen," she says. "He came back. He knows you're pissed. But he wants to know if you can come back and help us load the truck."

I laugh and order another beer.

So the next day, I'm sent to help another guy who has his own business, this one installing computer wires. When I show up on time and sober, he is prepared to take me on and make me a managing partner.

This is a common refrain, I'm starting to realize, from people who own their own businesses. They all want reliable help. But with most of them, I've learned, there's a reason why they don't have it. In Art's case, obviously, it would be pathological lying. In Ken's, I'm sure I'll find out.

The first day, honeymoon day, goes by wonderfully, as honey-moon days will. I drive from one office site to another and get down on my hands and knees under desks and change a few switch plates. Then all I'm required to do is wait by the switch plate while Ken goes off into a central wiring room and asks me over a walkie-talkie when the power comes on. Without a helper, he'd have to walk back and forth from the room to the switch plate every time he connected a new test line, so my merely being there and doing next to nothing is saving him tons of time. He mentions this over and over, obviously grateful for my assistance. Then he takes me to lunch.

"Just quit the temp service," he tells me. "I'm paying them fourteen an hour for you. They're giving you eight an hour. I'll give you ten and then we both make more money."

"Hey, that sounds good."

"Do you like to travel?" he asks.

"I love to."

"This job involves lots of travel."

Now we're getting dangerously close to classified ad bullshit. Travel can mean a lot of things. It can mean Rome and Paris, or it can mean sitting in a van on the interstate for six hours on our way to an office park upstate. I suspect the latter. But Ken seems like a straightforward guy, and I tell him that he doesn't need to sell me the job, I've already bought it. I've got nothing else going on right now, and learning a little about computer wiring might come in handy.

This gets him excited, and when we get back to the truck, he hands me a manual about a thousand pages thick, the bible of computer wiring. "Look that over," he tells me.

So I do. It's a thousand pages of incomprehensible drawings of resistors and capacitors and networks and interference wiring and hundreds of other terms I can't even begin to understand. This is a manual for electrical engineers, not for an English major who has expressed a mild interest in the field. I need something a little more like *Sesame Street*.

"Take that home with you," he says. "I don't expect you to understand it all in one day."

That's a relief. I put it between the seats. "So what happened to your last helper?" I ask.

"I've had about nine in the last five months," he tells me. "They just keep quitting. I've no idea why."

"Hmmmm."

"Sometimes the job gets really difficult. It's not all crawling around on office floors. Factory work can be a little sweaty sometimes. Some guys don't like that. How do you feel about it?"

"About breaking a sweat? It's not so bad. I'm used to it."

"It's a tough business," he says. "A lot of competition. You gotta push. Gotta work hard. You gotta kill yourself to survive."

The oxymoron seems lost on him. I nod in agreement. After Alaska, I don't think there's work out there that I couldn't keep up with.

He nods. "A lot of the guys I've had lately are just pussies, I guess."

I work with Ken for a week and everything is still going well. I still don't understand the electronic crap, but I'm excellent at carrying equipment around and using a walkie-talkie, which is most of what the job requires. He gets a contract to work at a factory, which is one hour away, and we leave every morning at six and return at six at night. Then I learn that Ken doesn't like to take weekends off.

"This is my business," he says. "I've got this contract. I need to have this finished on time or I lose money."

"So we just work ninety days in a row?"

"You can take days off now and then if you'd like."

So I realize that Ken's definition of a pussy is someone who wants a day off now and then. That's okay, he's committed to his work. I'm sure he'd be reasonable about it if I complained about the hours, so I decide to hold off complaining until I get really tired. In the meantime, the overtime will come in handy.

Summer has come around, and the factory is a cinder block structure with no air circulation inside. Part of the work involves drilling holes through the cinder blocks that we will pass computer wires through. At ground level, this is no problem, but most of the drilling has to be done about twenty feet in the air, right up near the roof, as the wires will be above the drop ceiling. Up near the roof it's like an oven. Drilling through a cinder block fire wall, while trying to keep your balance on a ladder as you're soaking yourself with sweat so that everything becomes slippery, is slow work.

Ken doesn't like slow work. "How long does it take to drill a hole?" he shouts up the ladder one day. Every time the drill gets going into the cinder block, the ladder starts to vibrate and I have to slow down, so I can only do a little at a time or I take a twenty-foot fall. I come down the ladder, covered in cinder block dust, and explain this to him.

"Are you scared of heights?" he asks with obvious disgust.

"I respect them."

He shakes his head and walks off. A plasterer nearby who has seen this comes over.

"That's dangerous as hell," he tells me. "You should be using a scaffold. I'm almost done with mine. You can wheel it over."

So an hour later, using the scaffold, I'm actually able to balance while pushing the drill through the block, and I get all eight holes drilled in a matter of minutes. I show my handiwork to Ken, who nods once and says, "Come on, we're running behind. I need help with this push rod in the roof."

This goes on for the rest of the week. No matter how quickly we get done, we're always running behind. By Friday evening, I've worked sixty hours.

"Can you work tomorrow?" Ken asks.

"I'd love a day off."

He thinks about this, then nods. "Okay. How about Sunday?"

I sigh. "All right. Sunday."

"If you worked tomorrow," he pushes, "it'd all be overtime. Sunday's the first day of the new week."

"I need a day off, Ken. I've about had it."

He thinks this over. "Okay, Sunday. I've got some work to do on another one-day job I can do tomorrow."

This guy's a hard worker, and I respect that, but I'm almost tempted to tell him to take it easy, that he's going to kill himself. I know he wouldn't listen. This is the type of guy who might one day own a million-dollar company—driven, ambitious, aggressive. I wouldn't begrudge him any of it. But me, I'm not looking to be a millionaire any time soon. I need a day off.

Sunday morning at six I show up at his place, and we drive out to the factory. Ken has me drive because on Saturday, my day off, he has worked twenty hours straight at the other job he needed to finish, so now he sacks out and gets a little bit of sleep. His eyes are red-rimmed and glassy as we set up the ladders and get to work, pushing wires around through the roof.

"Pull the wire," he shouts at me. We're in different rooms, about thirty feet apart, and I'm holding a mass of wires.

"Which one?"

"THE ONE I JUST GAVE YOU!" he bellows, furious. All the wires look the same, and I'm not sure which one he just slid through. I pull one.

"DAMNIT! Not that one. For Christ's sake!" And then I hear a short yell and the sound of a ladder collapsing.

I climb down and run into the next room, where Ken is lying

unconscious next to his ladder. I yell his name, try to get him to respond, but nothing. I run over to a phone and call an ambulance.

At the hospital, the doctor tells me Ken is lucky that he's not paralyzed from the waist down, and he's going to have to stay a few days. I call his mother, who drives three hours out to the hospital, and then I leave to load all the stuff back into the truck.

It's ironic that this man who works so hard for his independence now has to room with his mother. Those are the choices. That's the glamour of running your own business. Kill yourself to survive.

And that's the end of that career.

Vanishing Demographic

I decide I'm done moving around.

There's no dream job out there. It's the same for everyone. You've got to do something or you starve, and what it is really doesn't matter. At least there are jobs available, jobs that will keep your head above water, keep you one step ahead of the bill collector.

There are people who tell me they've found their dream job. Guys I'm sitting around getting drunk with will tell me that sometimes, the younger ones. But then three weeks later, I see them bartending. "So what happened to that great job you were telling me about?" I'll ask. They shrug. "Didn't work out."

I know enough not to even say the words anymore, so I don't have to be on the receiving end of that conversation. If I've got a job I can take for even a week, I consider myself blessed and I keep my mouth shut.

Go confidently in the direction of your dreams, Thoreau said. Later, he added that most men lead lives of quiet desperation, indicating that few, if any of us, were taking his advice. Fuck him, he had a trust fund. Who the hell else but a rich man could afford to spend a summer sitting by a lake thinking about life? I'll take the next thing that comes along and stick with it, because the looking, the hope that something better is out there, drains you of more energy than the drudgery itself.

Before I get the paper out again, I go out for a beer with the plasterer who lent me the scaffold. The whole plaster crew is there. It's Friday, payday for all of us, and we throw our money around as if it doesn't matter. It doesn't, is the lie we tell ourselves for the evening. I watch a guy place a $300 bet on a baseball game and act like the score of the game is of no consequence to him. We drink and talk while the game is on in the background, and he's quiet, sitting at the table, his back to the big screen TV. His team is getting crushed, the score is 10–1, it's over by the second inning.

"Eddie," one of the guys says, laughing. "You do that every fucking week." They get a kick out of this, watching him self-destruct, watching him piss his money away. You've got to be better than someone. Eddie stares into his beer.

"I don't care," he says.

I have no requirements for my new job except that it be free of bullshit. I don't want to hear about how all my dreams are about to come true, how I can be a millionaire in six weeks. I'd rather just hear that I get to work near a coffee-maker, or I get paid breaks.

"English degree?" the man says, looking quizzically at my

résumé. I'm going all out here, actually printing up a résumé. Résumé, the French term for "page full of bullshit," which glorifies three or four of the last forty-five jobs I've had and ignores the others. The few that I glorify are the ones where there are references who've agreed to lie for me, or that have gone out of business, or are in Alaska. No one will call Alaska to check a reference, I've learned. Don't ask me why.

I'm in the local office of the country's largest bug-spraying company, looking across a desk at a fat, wrinkled man staring at my résumé. The tiny office stinks of cigarette smoke, and there is ash on the cheap tiled floor. Behind him, the only decoration on the faded yellow wall is a single small plaque, honoring him as salesman of the year. It's a decade old. He lights another cigarette.

"Yes," I nod proudly. Or maybe not. I'm nodding anyway.

"I find that English graduates don't do well in this field," he tells me. "They tend to be too analytical."

That's great. Not only is my degree useless, it's a liability. A big part of this job is sales, as I'm not only supposed to spray, but I'm also supposed to convince the home owners to buy more and more pesticide. The idea is that I show up to give them a free squirt or two, then "find" hundreds of problems with their house, which more pesticide would solve. People can get rich doing this, I've just learned. There was a pre-interview introductory video that showed me how the top salesman last year made over $100,000.

My English degree is clearly a problem for him. He's actually making a face. I'm an experienced enough bullshitter that I could start waffling away, telling him all the things he wants to hear about how I could totally commit myself to convincing even the poorest home owner to spend thousands covering their house with poison, how I could be a loyal company man.

But I sit quietly. I know he's right. I should never have come here, I should never have put on this suit and sat with the others watching the video. Hire one of them, I should tell him.

But he goes on. "We don't provide company cars your first year," he tells me, "and there's a lot of driving. Do you have a reliable car?"

My car is about done. I'm lucky it got me to the interview. "Sure," I say. He doesn't want me, I don't want him, but neither one of us wants to admit it. The interview was over the minute he picked up my résumé, the minute I saw his dried out little body, wasted by years of cigarette smoke and poison-spraying, sitting behind his broken down desk in his faded excuse for an office, his reward for two decades of service. It reminds me of a holding cell. But we drag it out. He asks me a few more questions. I answer them. The phone rings, and he talks on it for a while as I look around his office. Maybe one day all this can be mine. Then he describes the job for a few more minutes.

"Thank you for coming in," he says finally, mercifully.

"Thank you very much."

"I'll call you."

"I'll wait by the phone."

I'm at a company that wants to hire people to install ATMs. There is a list of requirements for the job about a page long. Must have experience with computer installation, clean driver's license, clean credit, clean police record, clean urine. I don't have any of these things, but I figure neither does anyone else who answers an ad for a nine-dollar-an-hour job. They give me an application to fill out, and it's so long and asks so much personal information that I can't imagine anyone reads the answers. Most companies that make claims of thoroughness, I know, are less picky than the ones that don't. They hope the claims alone will keep the riffraff from applying.

This might be different, though. If I'm handling hundreds of thousands of dollars, maybe somebody is actually doing a background check. I look around the room and see a lot of clean-cut fresh faces, people with spotless backgrounds and pure hearts eager to earn survival money. I don't fit in here. I'm not pure enough. I walk out with my three-page application still unfinished and toss it in the trash by the door.

Big John at the moving company likes me. He wants me to start now, today. Most moving companies do. His eagerness makes me wary. He, too, it turns out, is an English graduate, and he wants to talk Shakespeare during the interview. Didn't I just love *As You Like It*? I nod vigorously. I'm not sure I remember which one that was. No matter, I'm sure he doesn't either. Perhaps at work we can discuss the finer points of Milton's *Paradise Lost* while struggling to get a sofa bed down the stairs.

Big John sees management possibilities for me. "After a while, we could have you supervise a crew," he tells me. "I only have two trucks right now, but I'm looking into getting a long-distance operation going. I need someone reliable to manage that." I nod politely. Why not? He seems like a nice fellow, clean cut, honest, obviously a hard worker. You wouldn't get into this business unless you were a hard worker. His rosy view of my future with his company is a flattering change from the last few interviews.

"I have a crew working on the other side of town right now," he tells me. "They could use some help." I'm not wearing a suit, I've given up on that, but even in slacks and a nice shirt, I'm hardly dressed for the rough and sweaty job of moving. I wasn't expecting to go to work a half hour after I walked into the office.

"Actually, I have a few errands I have to run this afternoon," I lie. My suspicions are deepening. I'm being flattered because he needs help today, immediately. He's got a warm body in his office who *might* want to work for him and he's not letting me out of here without a fight. I thought *I* was the one looking for something, and the tables have been turned on me. He looks at me, pleading.

"I've got two guys doing a fourteen-hour job," he says. "I could sure use your help."

"I'll try to wrap the errands up," I tell him tiredly. "And I have to go home and change."

Say what you like about hauling sofa beds down stairs in a North Carolina summer, it is free of bullshit. No one is telling me to smile and say, "Have a nice day." No one who is moving is having a nice day. When the job is over, there is some degree of satisfaction and the customers are usually grateful.

The management possibilities I heard so much about at the interview are a long way off, I soon discover. "In a few years, I'm getting another truck," Big John tells me one afternoon as we sit, dripping with sweat, on a customer's stairway. So now it's a few years. At the interview, it sounded like I was being promoted tomorrow because of the magical power of my English degree. Besides, there are half a dozen guys who work for this service, and there's no reason I should be the first in line for a supervisor's job. He's got his warm body, I've been here a few weeks, and I get less valuable every day. Moving is a summer sport; half the people who move do so between June and September, and September is creeping up on us. Soon Big John will be able to let half of us go. So the question isn't who is getting the supervisor position, which doesn't really exist, it's who's going to be collecting unemployment.

I know that him telling me this is just the bonding experience of two men who have just carried a brutally heavy object down three flights of stairs. I don't mind. I don't think I have two years of this in my future. It's not the physical punishment that drains me, it's the drudgery of every day being the same. A sofa bed. A bookcase. An armoire. Another sofa bed. And on and on. There's no skill to it that I haven't learned by my second week.

"Yeah," he repeats. "That'll be good, a second truck. With an ICC license, we could go long distance too. We need to get you a CDL, a tractor license."

"Sure, sounds good." I've heard this before, somewhere.

"Yeah." He stares off wistfully into the blazing sun as he swigs his water, imagining his fleet of trucks with "Big John's Moving" on the side, pulling into a giant, fenced-off yard. "I'll get all you guys licenses." Then he adds quickly, "Some time next year."

Some time next year. That's too long to wait. Aside from making me a liability at sales and a lot of other professions, a four-year university English degree has made me impatient at the few jobs I can get. It's filled me with a sense of entitlement. This makes it difficult to lug other people's crap around for any period of time while waiting for a promotion which, incidentally, I don't really want.

So to half the world I'm unemployable, and I'm not interested in the other half. They should have mentioned something about that at commencement, when they were telling us that we were the future of the world, the bright shining blah blah blah. Actually, I never made it to commencement because I already knew I'd been fucked by my third year and didn't feel like chasing bad money with good by renting a $100 gown and frying my ass off in the sun when I could be lying by a pool. The point is, by the end of my junior year, when job fairs were coming to the school to recruit graduates, I didn't see a single ad bearing the legend "English Degree Required."

There are plenty of ways to look at it. It's not so bad. I'm in the richest country in the world; even being broke here is better than being middle class in Peru or Angola. I could be a peasant in Senegal. That's it, that's the phrase they should tell you when they hand you an English degree at commencement, or a limp paycheck for pouring your energy into a meaningless, unsatisfying job for a faceless corporation. "Here you go. Congratulations. Hey, you could be a peasant in Senegal."

It's not the money. The real problem is with the expendability of us all. One human is as good as the next. Loyalty and effort are not rewarded. It's all about the bottom line, a phrase as loathsome to any worker as lay off or forced retirement. Granted, we've come a long way since they built the Hoover Dam, or since people died building the railways, but the corporate attitude toward the people who get things done is still the same. And the pendulum is swinging back the other way. The people who make the promises are so removed that they don't even realize anymore that the promises are meaningless. Stock shares in your company after five years? Great, thanks. But we both know that, statistically speaking, in five years, I'll be so long gone you wouldn't remember my face.

I watch football games and see endless commercials about retirement plans and investment portfolios, and I look around at the other people in the bar. Who are these commercials for? Not for anyone here. A long-term investment for these guys is next week's Monday Night Football—the Steelers and seven. These commercials used to be for beer and chips. I'm part of a demographic that is slipping off the radar.

I could write a book about this shit. So could a million others.

I grab the Sunday classifieds, get a cup of coffee, and sit down by the phone.